SAINSBURY'S

WOK AND STIR-FRY

JENI WRIGHT

NOTES

1. Standard level spoon measurements are used in all recipes.
1 tablespoon = one 15 ml spoon
1 teaspoon = one 5 ml spoon

2. Both metric and imperial measurements have been given in all recipes. Use one set of measurements only and not a mixture of both.

3. Eggs should be size 3 unless otherwise stated.

4. Pepper should be freshly ground black pepper unless otherwise stated.

5. Milk should be full-fat unless otherwise stated.

6. Fresh herbs should be used unless otherwise stated. If unavailable use dried herbs as an alternative but halve the quantities stated.

7. Servings given at the end of each recipe are calculated as part of a main meal. Rice or noodles and/or a vegetable or salad should be served as accompaniments.

8. Carbohydrates, fat and fibre are measured in grams for the nutritional information.

Published exclusively for
J Sainsbury plc
Stamford Street, London SE1 9LL
by Cathay Books, an imprint of Reed Consumer Books Limited
Michelin House, 81 Fulham Road, London SW3 6RB
and Auckland, Melbourne, Singapore and Toronto

First published 1990
Reprinted 1992, 1993, 1994

ISBN 0 86178 603 3

Produced by Mandarin Offset
Printed and bound in China

CONTENTS

INTRODUCTION

FOR LIGHT AND HEALTHY NUTRITIOUS COOKING, THERE IS NOTHING TO COMPARE WITH STIR-FRYING IN A WOK — AND IT'S QUICK AND EASY TOO! FRESH INGREDIENTS ARE COOKED OVER A HIGH HEAT FOR THE MINIMUM TIME IN A SMALL AMOUNT OF OIL. NUTRIENTS ARE RETAINED, ALONG WITH TEXTURE, COLOUR AND FLAVOUR.

Stir-frying is an ancient Chinese form of cooking. This simple, fast cooking method has now become enormously popular in the West as a modern, health-conscious way to cook.

THE WOK

The traditional Chinese wok is a simple, high-sided, round-bottomed cooking vessel. Made of carbon steel, it conducts heat very quickly, making it efficient and economical in the use of fuel.

Its shape allows you to toss and stir the food around over a high heat so that the food cooks evenly and in rapid time. All ingredients keep their natural colour and flavour. Because of the unique shape of the wok, only a very small amount of oil is needed to swirl around the bottom of the pan at the beginning of cooking. The wok is very versatile, it can be used for braising and deep-frying as well as for stir-frying – and even for steaming.

CHOOSING A WOK

Stir-frying can be done in a conventional, heavy-based frying pan, but the wok is best suited to the purpose of stir-frying, and authentic Chinese woks are very cheap. There is such a huge variety of woks, however, that it is bewildering for the novice cook to know which one to choose.

The simple, inexpensive Chinese type is one of the best buys. Available from supermarkets and Chinese and oriental hardware stores, they come without any fancy packaging. This type is round-bottomed and usually made of thin carbon steel (the best conductor of heat); it will be deep and feel heavy when picked up, and it should be at least 35 cm (14 inches) in diameter. Chinese woks are available with one handle (a pau wok) or with two short handles on either side (a Cantonese wok). The pau wok is intended for stir-frying as it can be held steady in one hand while the ingredients are tossed and turned with a spatula or scoop in the other. The two-handled Cantonese wok often has a slightly flatter bottom than the pau wok and is therefore more stable for deep-frying, braising and steaming. Newcomers to stir-frying often feel more comfortable stir-frying with a two-handled wok, however, because of its greater stability, but it is entirely up to you which one you choose.

Some woks have metal handles, but those with wooden handles are best. Metal handles become very hot during stir-frying so oven gloves should be worn, but they do not make for easy handling of the wok.

If possible avoid buying woks made of stainless steel as they do not conduct heat well – or non-stick woks, as these cannot be seasoned.

Gas hobs are best for stir-frying. If you do not have gas you can still stir-fry, but you will have to buy a wok with a flat bottom specifically designed for use on electric hobs. It is also possible to use a wok on a stand over an electric hob, but this method is not particularly successful as it slows down the cooking time and seems to defeat the whole object of stir-frying. This is also the case with electric woks, which do not reach a high enough temperature for successful stir-frying.

WOK ACCESSORIES

There are an enormous variety of 'accessories' available to go with woks, not all of which are essential. The following accessories are all that you need to cook any of the dishes in this book.

Spatula or scoop A very useful piece of equipment. It is a long-handled utensil like a shovel made of metal with a wooden end. Its shape is specially designed for tossing and turning the ingredients around the wok, and although an ordinary long-handled spoon or spatula can be used instead, they do not have quite the same action.

Wok lid Lids are not used for stir-frying, but if you plan to use your wok for steaming and braising, then you will need a lid. The high, dome-shaped variety is best, and these are usually sold separately.

Wok stand A stand is essential for deep-frying, steaming and braising, as it provides a secure and stable base – this is especially necessary if you are using a round-bottomed wok. Stands are made of metal and are either simple open-sided frames, or solid metal with holes around the sides.

Wok brush This is not essential. It is used by Chinese cooks for cleaning the wok and is made from sticks of bamboo bound together at the handle end with more bamboo. You can use an ordinary kitchen brush instead.

Bamboo steamer This fits inside the wok on a trivet and is used mainly for steaming fish and vegetables. Chinese bamboo steamers have the advantage that they can be stacked on top of each other so that several foods can be cooked at the same time. Unless you plan to do a lot of steaming in the wok this is really a luxury item.

Bamboo strainer A wide, flat metal strainer with a long bamboo handle which makes the lifting of foods in and out of the wok easier, especially when deep frying. An ordinary metal slotted spoon can be used instead.

CARING FOR YOUR WOK

If you have bought an authentic Chinese wok made of carbon steel, you will have to treat it before use; this process is called 'seasoning'. If the wok is from a Chinese hardware store it may well have a protective coating of oil over it, in which case this should be scrubbed off with a scourer, cream cleanser and hot water. Once this oil has been removed, place the wok over a low heat to become thoroughly dry and hot, then rub a little vegetable oil over the inside of the wok with a pad of kitchen paper; the paper will become black. Repeat this process several times until the paper is clean, then your wok will be ready for use. After cooking, wash the wok in very hot water, using a soapless scourer if necessary, then dry thoroughly. If not in constant use, a wok will soon become rusty. If this happens, simply scour off the rust and repeat the seasoning process.

TECHNIQUES FOR STIR-FRYING

While stir-frying is a quick-and-easy cooking method, it is essential to know how to prepare ingredients for cooking in order to be successful. It takes a little time and practice to perfect the techniques of slicing, cutting and chopping.

Choice of ingredients

All the ingredients used here are readily available. Where an unusual oriental ingredient is listed, a suitable alternative is suggested.

Because ingredients are cooked for the minimum time in a wok, they should be of the highest quality. Only the freshest of vegetables should be used, and only premium cuts of meat and poultry. Stir-frying brings out the natural quality of food and is therefore not suited to cheap cuts of meat, or vegetables that are past their best. This is not to say

that stir-frying is expensive. In the majority of recipes, you will find that only small quantities of meat, fish and poultry are used and that vegetables, noodles and rice are included to complement the protein.

Advance preparation

Before starting any stir-fry recipe, always read through the ingredients and method, then be sure to have all your ingredients ready prepared before cooking. Once you have begun cooking there will be no time for preparation of ingredients, blending cornflour, mixing sauces, and so on.

Advance preparation is helpful in that once everything is ready it can be left until just before you want to serve – ideal for entertaining. In addition to this, many recipes call for marinating which also allows time in between preparation and cooking. Minimum marinating times are given in recipes; if it is more convenient for you to marinate for longer, then by all means do so.

Slicing, cutting and chopping

Most oriental cooks use a cleaver to slice, cut, shred, mince and chop food, including bones. Although cleavers may look dangerous, they are easy to use, but you may prefer to use a knife.

In order that the ingredients cook as quickly as possible and absorb flavourings and seasonings in the very short cooking time, they should be cut into pieces of uniform size and thickness, and as many cut surfaces as possible should be exposed to the heat. Cutting and slicing techniques are therefore very important for stir-frying. Vegetables are usually cut on the diagonal or shredded; meat is cut across the grain, often in thin strips. Placing the meat in the freezer for about 1 hour beforehand makes it easier to cut wafer thin (once it is cut this way it defrosts almost immediately and is ready for cooking). You must use fresh meat when doing this and never refreeze meat that has already been frozen. While top-quality cuts are usually recommended, you will find economical ready prepared cuts which can also be used. 'Beef for stir-fries' and 'flash-fry steak' are two such cuts.

Preheating the wok and oil

Always heat a wok before putting anything in to

stir-fry (this helps prevent sticking), then add the oil and heat this over a moderate heat until hot. It is very important that the oil is hot, so that when food is added it will start cooking immediately. Take care when heating walnut, olive and sesame oils, however, as these have lower smoking points than groundnut and vegetable oils and can easily burn.

In many recipes, flavouring ingredients such as fresh root ginger, garlic and spring onions are added first, to flavour the oil before adding the main ingredients. If this is the case, turn the heat down to low or they will burn and become bitter. Once other ingredients are added, the heat can safely be increased to high and stir-frying proper can begin.

Adding ingredients to the wok

Always add ingredients to the wok in the order in which they are given in the recipe. Toss and turn the ingredients rapidly, working from the centre to the sides of the wok with a scoop or spatula. When adding a sauce or blended cornflour mixture, make a well in the centre of the ingredients then pour in the mixture and stir-fry vigorously over a high heat. If cornflour is used, make sure that the liquid boils for a thickened and glossy end result.

CHICKEN CHOP SUEY

CHOP SUEY ORIGINATED IN THE UNITED STATES AT THE TIME OF THE GOLD RUSH, WHEN THE FIRST CHINESE RESTAURANTS OPENED. THE NAME COMES FROM THE CHINESE WORD 'ZASUI' MEANING 'MIXED BITS'

2 teaspoons cornflour
4 tablespoons chicken stock or water
3 tablespoons soy sauce
2 tablespoons dry sherry or sherry vinegar
2 teaspoons soft dark brown sugar
¼ teaspoon salt
3 tablespoons groundnut or vegetable oil
4 spring onions, sliced diagonally into
   2.5 cm (1 inch) lengths
250 g (8 oz) button mushrooms, sliced thinly
3 carrots, cut into matchsticks
375 g (12 oz) cooked chicken, cut into
   bite-sized pieces
175 g (6 oz) frozen peas
1 × 227 g (8 oz) can sliced bamboo shoots,
   well drained

Blend the cornflour in a jug with 2 tablespoons of the stock or water, then add the remaining stock or water, the soy sauce, sherry or vinegar, sugar and salt. Stir well to combine.

Heat the wok until hot. Add the oil and heat over a moderate heat until hot. Add the spring onions and stir-fry over a gentle heat for 1-2 minutes to flavour the oil. Add the mushrooms and carrots, increase the heat to high and stir-fry for 2 minutes. Add the chicken and stir-fry for a further 2-3 minutes, then add the peas and bamboo shoots and toss well to mix. Pour in the cornflour mixture and bring to the boil over a high heat, stirring constantly until thickened and glossy. Stir-fry for 2 minutes or until the chicken has warmed through and is evenly coated in the sauce. Serve at once.

SERVES 4

Nutritional content per serving: Carbohydrate: 13   Fat: 15   Fibre: 3   Kilocalories: 290

Blending the cornflour.

Stir-frying the vegetables and chicken.

Stir-frying the mixture with the sauce.

Deep frying Deep frying in a wok is easier than you think. Because of the round bottom and deep, sloping sides of the wok, far less oil is needed than with a deep-fat fryer – for a dish to serve 4 people, 600 ml (1 pint) vegetable oil should be sufficient. Heat the oil according to the temperature stated in the recipe – in most cases this will be 190°C, 375°F or until a cube of bread browns in 30 seconds.

Important points to remember when deep frying in a wok are:
- Never deep fry in a wok without using a stand.
- Never exceed the recommended temperature or let the oil smoke.
- Always make sure that the food is thoroughly dried before adding to the hot oil.
- Never leave hot oil in the wok unattended.

SWEET AND SOUR PORK

THIS IS A MODERN VERSION OF THE WELL-KNOWN, CLASSIC CHINESE DISH. IT HAS A LIGHT, CRISPY BATTER AND A FRESH, FRUITY SAUCE

1 tablespoon cornflour
2 teaspoons soy sauce
500 g (1 lb) pork fillet (tenderloin), cut into bite-sized cubes
600 ml (1 pint) vegetable oil for deep frying
1 egg, beaten
SAUCE:
2 teaspoons cornflour
2 tablespoons water
1 × 227 g (8 oz) can pineapple slices in natural juice, drained and chopped, with juice reserved
2 tablespoons dry sherry or wine vinegar
2 tablespoons soft dark brown sugar
2 tablespoons soy sauce
1 tablespoon tomato purée or tomato ketchup
1 tablespoon groundnut or vegetable oil
1 small red pepper cored, deseeded and cut into strips
1 small green pepper cored, deseeded and cut into strips

Whisk the cornflour in a shallow dish with the soy sauce. Add the cubes of pork and stir well to mix. Cover and set aside.

Prepare the sauce: blend the cornflour in a jug with the water, then add the pineapple juice, sherry or vinegar, sugar, soy sauce and tomato purée or ketchup. Stir well to combine.

Heat the oil in a heavy-based saucepan. Add the pepper strips and fry for 2-3 minutes until slightly softened, stirring frequently. Pour in the cornflour mixture and bring to the boil over a high heat, stirring constantly until thickened and glossy. Stir in the chopped pineapple, cover and remove from the heat.

Place the wok on its stand on the hob. Pour the oil for deep frying into the wok and heat over a moderate heat to 190°C, 375°F or until a cube of bread browns in 30 seconds.

Add the beaten egg to the pork and stir to coat. Lift out a few cubes of pork with a slotted spoon and lower into the hot oil. Deep fry for 3-4 minutes until golden and crisp. Lift out with a slotted spoon and keep hot on kitchen paper while deep frying the remainder. Quickly reheat the sauce until bubbling. Place the cubes of pork in a warmed serving dish and pour over the sauce. Serve at once.

SERVES 4

Nutritional content per serving: Carbohydrate: 28   Fat: 40   Fibre: 2   Kilocalories: 580

Adding the pineapple to the sauce .

Removing the pork with a slotted spoon .

The finished dish .

Steaming Steaming is a very popular cooking method in oriental countries. It is one of the healthiest ways to cook, as no added fat is required and the natural flavour of good-quality ingredients can be fully appreciated.

The easiest way to steam in a wok is with a bamboo steamer (see the recipe for Sea Bass with Spring Onions and Ginger, below), but if you do not have a steamer, you can improvise: place the food to be steamed on a plate which will fit inside the wok. Place a metal or wooden trivet in the bottom of the wok and place the wok on its stand on the hob. Pour in enough boiling water to just cover the trivet, then place the plate on the trivet. Bring to the boil over a high heat, then lower the heat to a gentle simmer and cover the wok with its lid. Steam for the recommended time, then test to see if done and steam for a little while longer if necessary. Check the water level from time to time during steaming so that it does not boil dry.

SEA BASS WITH SPRING ONIONS AND GINGER

IF YOU HAVE A 35 CM (14 INCH) WOK, BUY A 33 CM (13 INCH) BAMBOO STEAMER TO FIT SNUGLY INSIDE. IF THE FISH ARE TOO LONG, CUT OFF THE HEADS AND PLACE THEM ALONGSIDE THE FISH. THEY CAN THEN BE REASSEMBLED FOR SERVING

2 × 500 g (I lb) whole sea bass, gutted, with heads and tails left on
I bunch spring onions, shredded
5 cm (2 inch) piece fresh root ginger, cut into matchsticks
3 tablespoons soy sauce
3 tablespoons dry sherry or sherry vinegar
I teaspoon caster sugar

Wash the fish inside and out, then pat dry with kitchen paper. Vandyke the tails by cutting in a 'V' shape with kitchen scissors, then make deep, diagonal slashes in each side of the fish with a sharp knife.

Place the fish on an oblong or oval platter that will fit inside your bamboo steamer. Put half of the spring onions and ginger inside the fish, then sprinkle the remainder on top.

Put the plate inside the bamboo steamer. Mix together the soy sauce, sherry or vinegar and sugar in a jug, then drizzle over the fish.

Place the wok on its stand on the hob. Cover the steamer with its lid, then place in the wok. Pour in enough boiling water to cover the base of the steamer, then bring to the boil over a high heat.

Lower the heat to a gentle simmer, cover the wok with its lid and steam for 15 minutes, checking the water level occasionally and topping up with more boiling water if necessary. Test to see if done (the flesh should look opaque near the bone) and steam for a little while longer if necessary.

SERVES 4-6

Nutritional content per serving: Carbohydrate: 4   Fat: 4   Kilocalories: 230

Cutting slashes in the sea bass.

Drizzling over the soy sauce mixture.

The steamer in the wok .

FISH AND SHELLFISH

FISH AND SHELLFISH ARE IMMENSELY VERSATILE INGREDIENTS, AS THIS CHAPTER ILLUSTRATES SO WELL. THEY CAN BE STIR-FRIED, DEEP FRIED, BRAISED OR STEAMED, AND WHICHEVER COOKING METHOD YOU CHOOSE, THE END RESULT WILL BE DELICIOUS AND EYE-CATCHING EVERY TIME.

PRAWN PUFFS

LEAVING THE TAILS ON THESE GIANT PRAWNS MAKES FOR EASY EATING WITH YOUR FINGERS: SIMPLY PICK THEM UP BY THEIR TAILS AND DIP THEM IN THE SAUCE

12 Mediterranean or large prawns
2 tablespoons plain flour, seasoned with salt
    and pepper
vegetable oil for deep frying
2 eggs
2 tablespoons very finely chopped spring
    onion
½ teaspoon Chinese five-spice powder
sweet and sour sauce and/or soy sauce for
    dipping

Peel the prawns with your fingers and remove the heads, keeping the tails on. Remove and discard the black veins. Cut each prawn in three lengthways without cutting right through at the tail end, so that the prawn remains intact. Rinse under cold running water, then pat dry thoroughly with kitchen paper. Coat in the seasoned flour.

Pour enough oil into the wok for deep frying and heat to 190°C, 375°F or until a cube of bread browns in 30 seconds. Meanwhile, beat the eggs in a bowl with the spring onion and five-spice powder.

When the oil is hot, dip the prawns into the egg mixture one at a time. Lift out with a spoon, making sure there is plenty of egg mixture around each prawn. Lower them gently into the hot oil and deep fry in batches for 1-2 minutes until crisp and light golden. Lift out with a slotted spoon, drain on kitchen paper and keep hot while deep frying the remainder. Serve at once as a first course with dipping sauces of your choice.

MAKES 12

Nutritional content per puff: Carbohydrate: 8   Fat: 11   Kilocalories: 170

SPICY FRIED FISH

5 cm (2 inch) piece fresh root ginger, peeled
    and chopped finely
1 clove garlic, crushed
3 tablespoons soy sauce
1 tablespoon lemon juice
pinch of chilli powder, or to taste
½ bunch spring onions, sliced diagonally into
    4 cm (1½ inch) lengths
500 g (1 lb) filleted monkfish, skinned and
    cut into 4 cm (1½ inch) chunks
2 tablespoons sesame oil
parsley sprigs to garnish

Whisk the ginger and garlic in a shallow bowl with the soy sauce, lemon juice, chilli powder and spring onions. Add the chunks of monkfish and turn gently to coat. Cover and leave to marinate for about 30 minutes, turning the fish occasionally.

Heat the wok until hot. Add the sesame oil and heat over a moderate heat until hot but not smoking. Remove a batch of monkfish pieces from the marinade with a slotted spoon, place in the wok and stir-fry for 5 minutes. Remove from the wok with the slotted spoon and keep warm while cooking the remaining monkfish in the same way.

When all the monkfish is cooked, pour any remaining marinade into the wok and simmer until hot. Pour over the monkfish and serve at once, garnished with parsley sprigs.

SERVES 4

Nutritional content per serving: Carbohydrate: 13   Fat: 9   Kilocalories: 120

Spicy Fried Fish; Prawn Puffs

CHILLI CRAB

1 cooked crab, weighing about 1.5 kg (2½ lb)
2.5 cm (1 inch) piece fresh root ginger, peeled and chopped roughly
1 clove garlic, chopped roughly
2 tablespoons groundnut or vegetable oil
½-1 teaspoon chilli powder, according to taste
4 tablespoons tomato ketchup
1 tablespoon chilli sauce
1 tablespoon soy sauce
1 tablespoon soft dark brown sugar
100 ml (3½ fl oz) boiling fish stock or water
salt
TO GARNISH:
cucumber slices
parsley sprigs

Place the crab on its back on a board. Twist off the claws and legs. Detach the body by holding the shell on the board with your fingers and pushing the body upwards with your thumbs. Pull away and discard the top shell, crab's mouth, stomach sac (this resembles a small crinkled bag and is near the mouth) and grey feathery gills known as 'dead men's fingers'.

Chop the crab shell and body in half with a cleaver or heavy knife, leaving the meat intact. Crack the claws open and crack the legs at the joints. Leave the meat inside both the claws and legs.

Pound the ginger and garlic to a paste in a pestle and mortar or with the end of a straight wooden rolling pin.

Heat the wok until hot. Add the oil and heat over a moderate heat until hot. Add the pounded mixture and the chilli powder and stir-fry over a gentle heat for 2-3 minutes to blend the flavours without browning the ingredients.

Add the tomato ketchup, chilli sauce, soy sauce and sugar and stir until boiling. Add the boiling fish stock or water, then the pieces of crab. Stir-fry for about 5 minutes until the crab is heated through, then taste the sauce and add salt if necessary. Serve hot, garnished with cucumber slices and parsley sprigs.

SERVES 2

Nutritional content per serving: Carbohydrate: 13   Fat: 12   Kilocalories: 220

QUICK-FRIED PLAICE WITH SPRING ONIONS

1 egg white
2 teaspoons cornflour
2 teaspoons sesame seeds
pinch of salt
375 g (12 oz) plaice fillets, cut into thin strips 4 cm (1½ inches) long
4 spring onions, sliced thinly on the diagonal
2.5 cm (1 inch) piece fresh root ginger, chopped
1 clove garlic, crushed
1 clove garlic, crushed
vegetable oil for shallow frying
SAUCE:
2 tablespoons soy sauce
1 tablespoon dry sherry or sherry vinegar
1 tablespoon lemon juice
1 teaspoon dark or light brown soft sugar
good pinch of Chinese five-spice powder

Blend the sauce ingredients together in a jug.

Lightly beat the egg white in a shallow dish with the cornflour, sesame seeds and salt. Add the strips of plaice and turn gently to coat.

Pour enough oil into the wok to come 2.5-4 cm (1-1½ inches) up the sides. Heat over a moderate heat until hot but not smoking. Shallow fry the plaice a few pieces at a time for about 2 minutes each batch or until golden. Lift out with a slotted spoon and drain on kitchen paper. Keep hot in a serving dish while cooking the remainder.

Carefully pour all but 1 tablespoon of oil out of the wok. Add the spring onions, ginger and garlic and stir-fry for 30 seconds, then pour in the sauce ingredients and bring to the boil over a high heat, stirring constantly. Pour the sauce over the plaice and serve at once.

SERVES 2-3

Nutritional content per serving: Carbohydrate: 14   Fat: 23   Kilocalories: 415

SESAME PRAWN TOASTS

THESE ARE A VERY POPULAR STARTER IN CHINESE RESTAURANTS. THEY ARE IDEAL SERVED HOT AS A LIGHT NIBBLE WITH DRINKS, AND ARE EQUALLY GOOD SERVED AS A TASTY AND NUTRITIOUS SNACK AT ANY TIME OF DAY. THEY TASTE EXTRA GOOD DIPPED INTO SOY SAUCE OR CHILLI SAUCE

1 large spring onion, chopped roughly

1-2 cloves garlic, chopped roughly

2.5 cm (1 inch) piece fresh root ginger, peeled and chopped roughly

250 g (8 oz) peeled cooked prawns, defrosted and dried thoroughly if frozen

2 tablespoons cornflour

2 teaspoons soy sauce

12 thin slices stale white bread

65 g (2½ oz) sesame seeds

vegetable oil for deep frying

Work the spring onion, garlic and ginger together in a food processor or blender with the prawns, cornflour and soy sauce until a smooth paste is formed.

Cut the crusts off each slice of bread, then cut each slice into 3 rectangular pieces. Spread the prawn paste evenly on 1 side of each slice of bread, then sprinkle with sesame seeds. Place in the refrigerator to chill for about 30 minutes.

Pour enough oil into the wok for deep frying and heat to 190°C, 375°F or until a cube of bread browns in 30 seconds. Deep fry the toasts a few at a time, paste side down, for 2-3 minutes each batch until golden brown.

Lift out the toasts with a slotted spoon and drain, paste side up, on kitchen paper while cooking the remainder. Serve the prawn toasts hot.

MAKES 36

Nutritional content per toast: Carbohydrate: 8   Fat: 10   Fibre: 1   Kilocalories: 135

Chilli Crab; Quick-Fried Plaice with Spring Onions; Sesame Prawn Toasts

STIR-FRIED PRAWNS WITH WATER CHESTNUTS AND MANGETOUT

THE CRISP, NUTTY TEXTURE OF WATER CHESTNUTS CONTRASTS WELL WITH THE SOFTNESS OF PRAWNS, AND THE COLOUR COMBINATION OF ALL THE DIFFERENT INGREDIENTS MAKES THIS A PRETTY DINNER PARTY DISH

2 tablespoons sesame seeds
1 tablespoon groundnut or vegetable oil
1 tablespoon sesame oil
1 bunch spring onions, sliced diagonally into 2.5 cm (1 inch) lengths
5 cm (2 inch) piece fresh root ginger, peeled and chopped finely
250 g (8 oz) mangetout
½ teaspoon salt
375 g (12 oz) peeled cooked prawns, defrosted and dried thoroughly if frozen
1 × 230 g (8 oz) can water chestnuts, drained and sliced thinly
3 tablespoons soy sauce
mint sprigs to garnish

Put the sesame seeds in the wok and dry-fry over a moderate heat for 1-2 minutes until toasted. Remove from the wok and set aside.

Add the groundnut or vegetable oil and the sesame oil to the hot wok. Heat over a moderate heat until hot but not smoking. Add the spring onions and ginger and stir-fry for 15 seconds. Add the mangetout and salt and stir-fry for 2 minutes, then add the prawns, water chestnuts and soy sauce. Increase the heat to high and stir-fry for a further 2 minutes. Garnish with mint sprigs then serve at once, sprinkled with the toasted sesame seeds.

SERVES 4

Nutritional content per serving: Carbohydrate: 16   Fat: 13   Fibre: 3   Kilocalories: 263

SCALLOPS IN GINGER CREAM

RICH AND CREAMY, THIS QUICK-COOKING DISH MAKES AN EXCELLENT MAIN COURSE FOR AN IMPROMPTU SUPPER PARTY. TO OFFSET THE RICHNESS, SERVE WITH PLAIN BOILED RICE AND A CRISP GREEN SALAD

1 large pinch saffron threads
2 tablespoons boiling water
8 shelled scallops, defrosted and dried thoroughly if frozen
2 tablespoons butter or margarine
1 tablespoon groundnut or vegetable oil
1 small onion, chopped finely
6 tablespoons dry white wine or dry vermouth or sherry
1 piece preserved stem ginger, with syrup, chopped finely
150 ml (¼ pint) double cream
salt and pepper
dill or chervil sprigs to garnish

Put the saffron threads in a heatproof bowl. Pour over the boiling water, stir and leave to soak.

Meanwhile, cut the scallops in half horizontally, detaching and reserving the coral.

Heat the wok until hot. Add the butter or margarine and oil and heat gently until foaming. Add the onion and stir-fry for 2 minutes or until softened. Strain in the saffron liquid. Pour in the wine, vermouth or sherry and bring to the boil over a high heat, then stir in the stem ginger. Add the scallops and stir-fry over a moderate heat for 3 minutes, then add the reserved coral and the cream and salt and pepper to taste. Stir-fry for a further 1 minute. Serve hot, sprinkled with dill or chervil sprigs.

SERVES 4

Nutritional content per serving: Carbohydrate: 4   Fat: 30   Kilocalories: 390

Stir-Fried Prawns with Water Chestnuts and Mangetout; Scallops in Ginger Cream; Crab Curry

CRAB CURRY

MONKFISH AND/OR PRAWNS CAN BE SUBSTITUTED FOR ALL OR SOME OF THE CRAB MEAT IN THIS LUXURIOUSLY RICH CURRY FROM INDONESIA. PLAIN BOILED WHITE RICE ACTS AS A FOIL, AND IS THE ONLY ACCOMPANIMENT NECESSARY

½ × 200 g (7 oz) packet creamed coconut
300 ml (½ pint) boiling water
50 g (2 oz) unsalted macadamia or cashew nuts, chopped finely
50 g (2 oz) desiccated coconut
1-2 fresh green chillies, according to taste
1 small onion, chopped roughly
5 cm (2 inch) piece fresh root ginger, peeled and chopped roughly
2 cloves garlic, chopped roughly
finely grated rind of 1 lemon, or 1 stem lemon grass
4 tablespoons groundnut or vegetable oil
1 teaspoon turmeric
white and dark meat from 1 large dressed crab
salt
fresh chopped coriander to garnish

Dissolve the creamed coconut in the boiling water to make coconut milk. Place the nuts in the wok with the desiccated coconut and dry-fry over a moderate heat for 1-2 minutes until toasted. Remove from the wok and set aside.

Roughly chop the chillies (discarding the seeds if you do not like a fiery hot curry). Pound the onion, ginger, garlic, chillies and lemon rind, if using, in a pestle and mortar or with the end of a straight wooden rolling pin.

Heat the wok until hot. Add the oil and heat over a moderate heat until hot. Add the pounded mixture and the turmeric and stir-fry over a gentle heat for 2-3 minutes to blend the flavours without browning the ingredients.

Add the dark crab meat and the coconut milk and increase the heat to moderate. Stir-fry for 2-3 minutes, then add the lemon grass, if using. Simmer for about 15 minutes or until thickened, stirring frequently. Discard the lemon rind or lemon grass.

Fold the white crab meat gently into the thickened sauce. Heat through gently, then taste and add salt if necessary. Serve hot, topped with the toasted coconut and nut mixture and garnished with chopped coriander.

SERVES 4

Nutritional content per serving: Carbohydrate: 10   Fat: 48   Fibre: 4   Kilocalories: 515

SPRING ROLLS

CHINESE SPRING ROLLS ARE TRADITIONALLY MADE WITH 'SPRING ROLL WRAPPERS'. THESE SPRING ROLLS ARE A WESTERN ALTERNATIVE USING FROZEN FILO PASTRY. IF THE FILO SPLITS DURING FILLING AND ROLLING, SIMPLY PATCH IT UP WITH EXTRA PIECES OF FILO

10 frozen filo pastry leaves, defrosted according to packet instructions
a little beaten egg for sealing
vegetable oil for deep frying
chilli sauce and/or soy sauce for dipping

FILLING:

2 tablespoons sesame oil
4 spring onions, trimmed and chopped coarsely
2.5 cm (1 inch) piece fresh root ginger, peeled and chopped finely
1 carrot, grated coarsely
300 g (10 oz) bean sprouts
250 g (8 oz) peeled cooked prawns, defrosted and dried thoroughly if frozen, chopped roughly
1 tablespoon soy sauce
salt and pepper

First make the filling. Heat the wok until hot. Add the sesame oil and heat over a moderate heat until hot but not smoking. Add the spring onions and ginger and stir-fry for 15 seconds. Add the carrot and bean sprouts and stir-fry for 2 minutes. Add the prawns and soy sauce, increase the heat to high and stir-fry for a further 2 minutes. Turn the mixture into a bowl, season to taste with salt and pepper, cover and leave to cool.

Trim each sheet of filo pastry into a 20-25 cm (8-10 inch) square. Divide the filling into 10 equal portions. Place 1 filo pastry square on a board, arranging it so that it faces you in a diamond shape. Place 1 portion of filling on the filo pastry, just a little below the centre. Fold up the bottom point of the diamond over the filling, then roll up the filo pastry around the filling, tucking in the 2 sides halfway. Brush the underside of the exposed point with egg and press to seal. Repeat with the remaining filo pastry filling to make a total of 10 spring rolls.

Wipe the wok clean with kitchen paper. Pour in enough oil for deep frying and heat to 180°C, 350°F or until a cube of bread browns in 40 seconds. Deep fry the spring rolls 3-4 at a time for 4-5 minutes each batch, or until the pastry is golden brown and crisp. Lift out with a slotted spoon and drain on kitchen paper while deep frying the remainder. Serve hot as a first course, with several dipping sauces of your choice.

MAKES 10

Nutritional content per roll: Carbohydrate: 4   Fat: 9   Kilocalories: 120

Spring Rolls; Hot Prawns

HOT PRAWNS

SIMPLE AND QUICK, THIS CHILLI-HOT DISH TRADITIONALLY USES RAW PRAWNS. HERE IT IS MADE WITH LARGE FRESH COOKED PRAWNS
WHICH ARE ONLY STIR-FRIED FOR 1-2 MINUTES SO THAT THEY REMAIN JUICY AND TENDER

2 tablespoons groundnut or vegetable oil

½ medium onion, sliced thinly

2.5 cm (1 inch) piece fresh root ginger, peeled and sliced thinly

1-2 cloves garlic, sliced thinly

500 g (1 lb) large cooked prawns, peeled, rinsed and dried

1½ tablespoons chilli powder

½ teaspoon salt

6 ripe tomatoes, skinned and cut into eighths

2-3 tablespoons chopped fresh coriander to garnish

Heat the wok until hot. Add 1 tablespoon oil and heat over a moderate heat until hot. Add the sliced onion, ginger and garlic and stir-fry over a gentle heat for 2-3 minutes to blend the flavours without browning the ingredients.

Add the prawns, chilli powder and salt. Increase the heat to high and stir-fry for 1-2 minutes. Tip all the ingredients out of the wok into a bowl, cover and set aside.

Heat the remaining oil in the wok over a moderate heat until hot. Add the tomatoes and stir-fry for several minutes until the juices run. Return the prawn mixture to the wok and stir-fry over a high heat for about 30 seconds until heated through. Serve hot, sprinkled with chopped coriander.

SERVES 4

Nutritional content per serving: Carbohydrate: 6   Fat: 9   Fibre: 2   Kilocalories: 200

TEN-VARIETY FRIED RICE

THIS THAI-STYLE DISH DERIVES ITS NAME FROM THE FACT THAT IT HAS 10 INGREDIENTS IN ADDITION TO RICE. YOU CAN VARY THESE ACCORDING TO WHAT YOU HAVE TO HAND – THERE ARE NO HARD-AND-FAST RULES

125-175 g (4-6 oz) fresh chicken breast fillets
125-175 g (4 -6 oz) fresh pork fillet
  (tenderloin)
2 eggs
2½ tablespoons groundnut or vegetable oil
1 large red pepper, cored, deseeded and
  chopped finely
4 spring onions, chopped finely
3 tomatoes, skinned and chopped roughly
2 cloves garlic, crushed
3 fresh green chillies, chopped roughly, seeds
  discarded according to taste
250 g (8 oz) cooked peeled prawns, defrosted
  if frozen
4 frozen crab sticks, defrosted and cut into
  bite-sized pieces
175 g (6 oz) long-grain white rice, boiled and
  drained
salt and pepper
chopped spring onions to garnish
SAUCE:
150 ml (¼ pint) fish or chicken stock
2 tablespoons soy sauce
1 tablespoon tomato ketchup
1 tablespoon caster sugar
2 teaspoons lemon juice
2 teaspoons anchovy essence

Wrap the chicken and pork and place in the freezer for about 1 hour, or until just frozen.

Meanwhile, make a flat omelette. Beat together the eggs and salt and pepper to taste. Heat 1 ½ teaspoons oil in a frying pan and add the eggs. As the edge begins to set, draw the mixture towards the centre and, at the same time, tilt the pan slightly allowing the uncooked egg to run from the centre on to the hot base of the pan to set quickly. Cook until the omelette is browned underneath and soft on top. Slide the omelette out of the pan on to a plate or board and roll up tightly; set aside. Blend the sauce ingredients together in a jug.

Cut the chicken and pork into thin strips. Heat the wok until hot. Add the remaining oil and heat over a moderate heat until hot. Add the chicken and pork, increase the heat to high and stir-fry for 2-3 minutes until browned on all sides, then add the prepared vegetables one at a time and stir-fry for 1-2 minutes after each addition. Add the prawns and crab sticks and stir-fry for 2-3 minutes more until hot, then add the rice and sauce mixture and toss well to mix. Add salt and pepper to taste, then stir-fry for a further few minutes until the rice is hot. Slice the omelette into thin strips and place on top of the rice mixture. Serve at once, garnished with chopped spring onions.

SERVES 4

Nutritional content per serving:	Carbohydrate: 8	Fat: 17	Fibre: 12	Kilocalories: 420

Ten-Variety Fried Rice; Sweet and Sour Fish

SWEET AND SOUR FISH

1 egg white
2 teaspoons cornflour
pinch of salt
500 g (1 lb) filleted cod or haddock, skinned
  and cut into 2.5 cm (1 inch) chunks
vegetable oil for deep frying
parsley sprigs to garnish
SAUCE:
1 tablespoon cornflour
125 ml (4 fl oz) fish stock or water
1 tablespoon soy sauce
1 tablespoon dry sherry or sherry vinegar
1 tablespoon cider vinegar
1 tablespoon soft dark or light brown sugar
1 tablespoon tomato purée
1 teaspoon French mustard

Lightly beat the egg white in a shallow dish with the cornflour and salt. Add the chunks of fish and turn gently to coat. Set aside.

Prepare the sauce: blend the cornflour in a jug with 2 tablespoons of the stock or water, then add the remaining stock or water and the remaining sauce ingredients. Stir well to combine.

Pour enough oil in the wok for deep frying and heat to 180°C-190°C, 350°F-375°F or until a cube of bread browns in 30 seconds. Deep fry the fish chunks a few at a time for 2-3 minutes each batch until golden. Lift out with a slotted spoon and drain on kitchen paper while deep frying the remainder.

Carefully pour the oil out of the wok. Pour in the sauce mixture and bring to the boil over a high heat, stirring constantly until thickened and glossy. Lower the heat, add the fish and simmer gently for 30 seconds to 1 minute until heated through. Garnish and serve at once.

SERVES 4

Nutritional content per serving: Carbohydrate: 8   Fat: 16   Kilocalories: 270

PRAWNS IN COCONUT MILK

COCONUT 'MILK' CAN BE MADE IN MANY DIFFERENT WAYS: WITH FRESH COCONUT, BLOCKS OR CANS OF CREAMED COCONUT, OR WITH DESICCATED COCONUT. THIS RECIPE USES DESICCATED COCONUT AND BOILING WATER, AN INEXPENSIVE METHOD, BUT DELICIOUSLY CREAMY NONETHELESS

25 g (1 oz) desiccated coconut
150 ml (¼ pint) boiling water
2 tablespoons groundnut or vegetable oil
2 celery sticks, sliced thinly on the diagonal
4 spring onions, sliced thinly on the diagonal
1 clove garlic, crushed
1 teaspoon ground coriander
1 teaspoon ground cumin
½ teaspoon ground ginger
½ teaspoon turmeric
½-1 teaspoon chilli powder, according to
  taste
1 tablespoon tomato purée
500 g (1 lb) cooked peeled prawns, defrosted
  and dried thoroughly if frozen
2 tablespoons chopped fresh mint
½ teaspoon salt or to taste
mint sprigs to garnish

Put the coconut in a bowl, pour in the boiling water and stir well to mix. Leave to stand for about 30 minutes.

Heat the wok until hot. Add the oil and heat over a moderate heat until hot. Add the celery, onions and garlic and stir-fry for 30 seconds. Add the spices and stir-fry for a further 30 seconds, then remove the wok from the heat.

Pour the coconut mixture into the wok through a fine sieve and press with the back of a metal spoon to extract as much milk as possible. Stir in the tomato purée, return the wok to a high heat and bring to the boil, stirring. Simmer for 5-10 minutes until thickened, stirring frequently.

Add the prawns to the coconut mixture and stir-fry for 1-2 minutes until heated through. Add the chopped mint and salt then taste and add more chilli powder if liked. Serve hot, garnished with mint sprigs.

SERVES 4

Nutritional content per serving: Carbohydrate: 3   Fat: 13   Fibre: 2   Kilocalories: 220

HONEYED PRAWNS

1 fresh red chilli
1 fresh green chilli
1 tablespoon groundnut or vegetable oil
2.5 cm (1 inch) piece fresh root ginger,
  peeled and chopped finely
250 g (8 oz) peeled cooked prawns, defrosted
  and dried thoroughly if frozen
salt and pepper
SAUCE:
2 teaspoons cornflour
4 tablespoons cold fish stock or water
2 tablespoons clear honey
1 tablespoon soy sauce

Slice the chillies crossways into thin rings, then rinse under cold running water to remove the seeds. Dry on kitchen paper.

Prepare the sauce: blend the cornflour in a jug with 1 tablespoon of the stock or water, then add the remaining stock or water and the remaining sauce ingredients. Stir well to combine.

Heat the wok until hot. Add the oil and heat over a moderate heat until hot. Add the ginger, chillies and prawns and stir-fry for 30 seconds. Pour in the sauce mixture and bring to the boil over a high heat, stirring constantly until thickened and glossy. Add salt and pepper to taste and serve at once.

SERVES 2

Nutritional content per serving: Carbohydrate: 20   Fat: 10   Kilocalories: 250

Prawns in Coconut Milk; Honeyed Prawns; Shanghai Smoked Fish

SHANGHAI SMOKED FISH

THIS DISH IS SO CALLED BECAUSE IT HAS THE APPEARANCE AND FLAVOUR OF SMOKED FISH, ALTHOUGH IT IS NOT SMOKED AT ALL

2.5 cm (1 inch) piece fresh root ginger, peeled and chopped finely
2 tablespoons dry sherry or sherry vinegar
2 tablespoons soy sauce
2 teaspoons soft dark brown sugar
½ teaspoon Chinese five-spice powder
¼ teaspoon salt
4 × 125 g (4 oz) plaice fillets, halved lengthways
100 ml (3½ fl oz) boiling water
2 egg whites
4 teaspoons cornflour
vegetable oil for shallow frying
chopped parsley to garnish

Whisk the ginger in a shallow dish with the sherry or sherry vinegar, soy sauce, sugar, five-spice powder and salt. Add the pieces of fish and spoon over the marinade. Cover and leave to marinate in the refrigerator for 1-2 hours, spooning the marinade over the fish occasionally.

When ready to cook, carefully lift the pieces of fish out of the marinade with a fish slice, pat dry with kitchen paper and set aside.

Pour the marinade into the wok, stir in the boiling water and bring to the boil. Simmer for about 10 minutes until thickened, stirring frequently. Strain into a bowl and keep warm. Wipe the wok clean with kitchen paper.

Lightly beat the egg whites in a shallow dish with the cornflour. Add the pieces of plaice and turn gently to coat. Pour enough oil into the wok to come 2.5-4 cm (1-1½ inches) up the sides. Heat over a moderate heat until hot but not smoking. Carefully lower the plaice, skin side up, into the wok. Shallow-fry a few pieces at a time for 4-5 minutes each batch, turning the plaice over once. Lift out with a slotted spoon and drain on kitchen paper, then arrange on a serving platter. Pour over the marinade and leave to cool. Garnish with chopped parsley and serve at room temperature.

SERVES 4

Nutritional content per serving: Carbohydrate: 7   Fat: 16   Kilocalories: 280

Braised whole fish with black bean sauce

Sea bass is very popular in Chinese cooking, but it is not available all year round. If you have difficulty in obtaining it, you can use grey mullet or trout instead. If only small fish are available, use two fish instead of the one suggested here

1 × 750 g (1½ lb) whole sea bass, gutted, with head and tail left on

a little plain flour, seasoned with salt and pepper, for coating

vegetable oil for shallow frying

6 spring onions, chopped finely

2 cloves garlic, crushed

125 ml (4 fl oz) fish or chicken stock

4 tablespoons black bean sauce

2 tablespoons soy sauce

2 tablespoons dry sherry or sherry vinegar

3 spring onions, green parts only, sliced on the diagonal, to garnish

Wash the fish thoroughly inside and out, then pat dry with kitchen paper. Coat the fish lightly with seasoned flour, shaking off any excess.

Pour enough oil into the wok to come 2.5-4 cm (1-1½ inches) up the sides. Heat over a moderate heat until hot but not smoking.

Carefully lower the fish into the hot oil. Shallow fry for 2 minutes, then turn over carefully and shallow fry for 2 minutes on the other side. Lift out of the oil and leave to drain on kitchen paper.

Meanwhile, carefully pour all but 1 tablespoon of oil out of the wok. Add the spring onions and garlic and stir-fry over a gentle heat for 2-3 minutes to blend the flavours without browning the ingredients.

Stir in the stock, the black bean and soy sauces and the sherry or vinegar. Bring to the boil, stirring, then return the fish to the wok. Cover and braise for 12 minutes, or until the flesh is opaque, basting frequently with the sauce.

Carefully remove the fish from the sauce and place on a warmed serving platter. Pour the sauce over the fish so that the spring onions are on top. (If you like, you can remove the skin of the fish first). Garnish with spring onions and serve at once.

SERVES 3-4

| Nutritional content per serving: | Carbohydrate: 6 | Fat: 24 | Fibre: 1 | Kilocalories: 420 |

Braised Whole Fish with Black Bean Sauce; Fish Balls with Broccoli and Mushrooms

FISH BALLS WITH BROCCOLI AND MUSHROOMS

600 ml (1 pint) fish or vegetable stock
3 spring onions, chopped roughly
3 cloves garlic, 2 of them crushed
1 tablespoon lemon juice
175-250 g (6-8 oz) broccoli, florets separated,
  stalks sliced thinly on the diagonal
125 g (4 oz) small button mushrooms
2 teaspoons cornflour
2 tablespoons water
2 tablespoons soy sauce
2 tablespoons dry sherry or sherry vinegar
2 tablespoons groundnut or vegetable oil
chives to garnish
FISH BALLS:
500 g (1 lb) filleted cod or other white fish
1 egg white
2 teaspoons cornflour
2 teaspoons groundnut or vegetable oil
2 tablespoons finely chopped fresh coriander
  or parsley
salt and pepper

First make the fish balls: skin the fish and remove any bones. Place the fish in a food processor or blender and work until smooth. Add the egg white, cornflour, oil, coriander or parsley and salt and pepper to taste. Work again until evenly blended. Form the mixture into about 36 small balls, place on a plate, cover and leave in the refrigerator to chill for 30 minutes.

Bring the stock to the boil in a saucepan with the spring onions, the whole clove garlic and the lemon juice. Boil for 5 minutes, then strain. Return the strained liquid to the pan and bring back to the boil, then drop in the fish balls. Simmer for 5 minutes, stirring several times, then lift out with a slotted spoon and drain in a colander.

Add the broccoli and mushrooms to the boiling stock and simmer for 2 minutes. Drain, reserving 8 tablespoons of cooking liquid. Blend the cornflour with the water. Add the reserved cooking liquid, the soy sauce and the sherry or vinegar. Stir well to combine.

Heat the wok until hot. Add the oil and heat over a moderate heat until hot. Add the fish balls and crushed garlic and stir-fry for 2 minutes. Add the broccoli and mushrooms, then pour in the cornflour mixture and bring to the boil over a high heat, stirring constantly until thickened and glossy. Taste the sauce, adjust the seasoning if necessary, and garnish with chives before serving.

SERVES 4-6

Nutritional content per serving: Carbohydrate: 14   Fat: 11   Fibre: 3   Kilocalories: 220

Beef

Tender cuts of beef lend themselves beautifully to the rapid method of stir-frying. Beef combines perfectly with a whole range of ingredients from oyster sauce to mango. It quickly absorbs the flavours of complementary seasonings to create a variety of succulent dishes.

STIR-FRIED BEEF WITH CELERY AND WALNUTS

ORANGE JULIENNE LOOKS GOOD AS A GARNISH ON THIS TASTY STIR-FRY. SIMPLY REMOVE THE RIND FROM AN ORANGE WITH A VEGETABLE PEELER, THEN CUT INTO VERY THIN MATCHSTICK STRIPS. BLANCH THE ORANGE RIND IN BOILING WATER FOR 1 MINUTE, RINSE IN COLD WATER AND PAT DRY

375 g (12 oz) rump or flash-fry steak
1 large orange
2 teaspoons cornflour
4 tablespoons cold beef stock or water
4 tablespoons orange juice
2 teaspoons Worcestershire sauce
2 teaspoons tomato purée
2 tablespoons groundnut or vegetable oil
1 onion, sliced thinly
4 celery sticks, sliced thinly on the diagonal
50 g (2 oz) walnut pieces
salt and pepper
celery leaves to garnish

Wrap the steak and place in the freezer for about 1 hour, or until just frozen, then cut into thin strips (across the grain if using rump steak, and discarding any fat and sinew).

Remove the skin and all white pith from the orange, then cut between the membranes to divide the orange neatly into segments.

Blend the cornflour in a jug with 1 tablespoon of the stock or water, then add the remaining stock or water, the orange juice, Worcestershire sauce and tomato purée. Stir well to combine.

Heat the wok until hot. Add the oil and heat over a moderate heat until hot. Add the onion and celery and stir-fry over a gentle heat until slightly softened. Add the meat, increase the heat to high and stir-fry for 3-5 minutes until browned on all sides. Pour in the cornflour mixture and bring to the boil over a high heat, stirring constantly until thickened and glossy. Remove from the heat and stir in the orange segments, walnuts and salt and pepper to taste. Garnish with celery leaves and serve at once.

SERVES 4

Nutritional content per serving: Carbohydrate: 5   Fat: 27   Fibre: 2   Kilocalories: 335

TERIYAKI BEEF STIR-FRY

TERIYAKI MARINADE IS A BOTTLED JAPANESE SAUCE MADE FROM NATURALLY BREWED SOY SAUCE, WINE AND SPICES

500 g (1 lb) fillet steak
5 cm (2 inch) piece fresh root ginger, peeled
  and chopped roughly
3 cloves garlic, chopped roughly
6 black peppercorns
6 tablespoons teriyaki marinade
4 tablespoons sweet sherry
2 tablespoons caster sugar
2 tablespoons groundnut or vegetable oil
1 spring onion, green part only, sliced thinly
  on the diagonal, to garnish

Wrap the steak and place in the freezer for about 1 hour, or until just frozen, then cut into thin strips across the grain, discarding any fat.

Crush the ginger and garlic with the peppercorns in a pestle and mortar. Whisk the ginger, garlic and peppercorns in a bowl with the teriyaki marinade, sherry and sugar. Add the slices of steak and stir well to mix. Cover and leave to marinate in the refrigerator for 24 hours, turning the meat occasionally.

When ready to cook, allow the meat to come to room temperature for about 1 hour. Heat the wok until hot. Add the oil and heat over a moderate heat until hot. Remove the meat from the marinade with a slotted spoon, add to the wok and increase the heat to high. Stir-fry for 1 minute, then pour over the marinade. Stir-fry for a further 1 minute until the mixture is hot. Garnish with spring onion and serve at once.

SERVES 4

Nutritional content per serving: Carbohydrate: 10   Fat: 36   Kilocalories: 460

Stir-Fried Beef with Celery and Walnuts; Teriyaki Beef Stir-Fry (bottom)

BEEF WITH OYSTER SAUCE

THIS IS A CLASSIC CANTONESE DISH. BOTTLED OYSTER SAUCE IS RICH, DARK AND HIGHLY CONCENTRATED IN FLAVOUR; IT IS MADE FROM OYSTERS, SOY SAUCE AND BRINE

500 g (1 lb) rump or flash-fry steak
2 cloves garlic, crushed
3 tablespoons soy sauce
2 tablespoons dry sherry or sherry vinegar
2 teaspoons cornflour
1 teaspoon caster sugar
2 tablespoons groundnut or vegetable oil
300 g (10 oz) Chinese leaves, shredded finely
5 spring onions, sliced thinly on the diagonal
2.5 cm (1 inch) piece fresh root ginger,
   peeled and cut into matchsticks
½ teaspoon salt
pepper
2 tablespoons oyster sauce

Wrap the steak and place in the freezer for about 1 hour, or until just frozen, then cut into thin slices (across the grain if using rump steak, and discarding any fat and sinew).

Whisk the garlic in a bowl with the soy sauce, sherry or vinegar, cornflour, sugar and plenty of pepper. Add the slices of steak and stir well to mix. Cover and leave to marinate for 20-30 minutes, turning the meat occasionally.

Heat the wok until hot. Add 1 tablespoon oil and heat over a moderate heat until hot. Add the Chinese leaves, spring onions, ginger and salt and stir-fry for 1½ minutes or until the Chinese leaves are just beginning to wilt. Remove the Chinese leaf mixture with a slotted spoon and keep warm.

Heat the remaining oil in the wok. Remove about one-quarter of the meat from the marinade with a slotted spoon and add to the wok. Increase the heat to high and stir-fry for 2-3 minutes until the meat is browned on all sides. Remove with a slotted spoon and set aside on a plate. Repeat with the remaining meat, stir-frying it in batches.

Add the oyster sauce and the marinade to the wok and bring to the boil over a high heat, stirring constantly until thickened and glossy. Return the meat and juices and the Chinese leaf mixture to the wok and stir-fry for about 30 seconds, or until all the ingredients are evenly combined and coated in the sauce. Serve at once.

SERVES 4

Nutritional content per serving:	Carbohydrate: 5	Fat: 25	Fibre: 2	Kilocalories: 360

Beef with Oyster Sauce; Pineapple Beef

PINEAPPLE BEEF

WHEN FRESH PINEAPPLE IS NOT IN SEASON, USE CANNED SLICED PINEAPPLE IN NATURAL JUICE

500 g (1 lb) rump steak

2.5 cm (1 inch) piece fresh root ginger, peeled and chopped finely

3 tablespoons groundnut or vegetable oil

2 tablespoons soy sauce

2 teaspoons soft dark brown sugar

¼ teaspoon Chinese five-spice powder

2 teaspoons cornflour

4 tablespoons cold beef stock or water

2 tablespoons dry sherry or sherry vinegar

4 slices fresh pineapple, cut into thin chunks

½ bunch spring onions, sliced diagonally into 4 cm (1½ inch) lengths

parsley sprigs to garnish

Wrap the steak and place in the freezer for about 1 hour, or until just frozen, then cut into 5 cm (2 inch) long slices across the grain, discarding any fat and sinew.

Whisk the ginger in a bowl with 1 tablespoon oil, 1 tablespoon soy sauce, the sugar and five-spice powder. Add the slices of steak and stir well to mix. Cover and leave to marinate for 20-30 minutes, turning the meat occasionally.

Blend the cornflour in a jug with 1 tablespoon of the stock or water, then add the remaining stock or water, the sherry or vinegar and the remaining soy sauce. Stir well to combine.

Heat the wok until hot. Add the remaining oil and heat over a moderate heat until hot. Add about one-quarter of the meat and increase the heat to high. Stir-fry for 2-3 minutes until the meat is browned on all sides. Remove with a slotted spoon and set aside on a plate. Repeat with the remaining meat, stir-frying it in batches.

Return all the meat and juices to the wok, pour in the cornflour mixture and bring to the boil over a high heat, stirring constantly until thickened and glossy. Add the pineapple and spring onions and stir-fry for about 30 seconds or until heated through. Garnish with parsley sprigs and serve at once.

SERVES 4

Nutritional content per serving: Carbohydrate: 12   Fat: 29   Fibre: 1   Kilocalories: 410

SIZZLING STEAK WITH MANGO

THE CONTRAST BETWEEN THE PEPPERY HOTNESS OF THE STIR-FRIED BEEF AND THE REFRESHINGLY COOL MANGO MAKES THIS DISH TANTALIZING TO THE TASTE BUDS. FOR A CHANGE, MELON, PAWPAW OR PINEAPPLE CAN BE SUBSTITUTED FOR THE MANGO

375 g (12 oz) fillet steak
4 black peppercorns
4 tablespoons olive or walnut oil
3 tablespoons dark rum
2 tablespoons lime juice
2 tablespoons chilli sauce
¼ teaspoon ground mixed spice
1 ripe mango
pinch of salt

Wrap the steak and place in the freezer for about 1 hour, or until just frozen, then cut into thin strips across the grain, discarding any fat and sinew. Crush the peppercorns in a pestle and mortar or grind in a pepper mill.

Whisk 2 tablespoons of the oil in a bowl with the rum, lime juice, chilli sauce, crushed peppercorns and mixed spice. Add the slices of steak and stir well to mix. Cover and leave to marinate for about 4 hours, turning the meat occasionally.

About 15 minutes before cooking, prepare the mango: peel with a knife, then cut a slice lengthways from each side of the fruit, taking the knife as close to the central stone as possible. Slice these 2 pieces of mango thinly, then cut as much flesh as possible away from the stone and slice this neatly.

Heat the wok until hot. Add the remaining oil and heat over a moderate heat until hot but not smoking. Add the meat and marinade, increase the heat to high and stir-fry for 2 minutes or until the meat is browned on all sides. Add the mango slices and salt and stir-fry for about 30 seconds or until heated through. Serve at once.

SERVES 4

Nutritional content per serving: Carbohydrate: 10   Fat: 36   Fibre: 1   Kilocalories: 450

BEEF RENDANG

BLOCKS OF CREAMED COCONUT ARE AVAILABLE IN PACKETS READY FOR DISSOLVING IN BOILING WATER

2 cloves garlic, chopped roughly
2.5 cm (1 inch) piece fresh root ginger, peeled and chopped roughly
2 dried red chillies
150 g (5 oz) creamed coconut
450 ml (¾ pint) boiling water
1 teaspoon turmeric
½ teaspoon salt
500 g (1 lb) rump steak, trimmed of fat and sinew and cut into bite-sized chunks
1 bay leaf
TO GARNISH:
desiccated coconut
bay leaves

Pound the garlic and ginger with the chillies in a pestle and mortar or with the end of a straight wooden rolling pin. Dissolve the creamed coconut in the boiling water to make coconut milk. Stir in the turmeric and salt. Put the meat and pounded mixture in the wok. Pour in the coconut milk and bring to the boil over a moderate heat, stirring constantly. Lower the heat, add the bay leaf and simmer gently for about 30 minutes or until the sauce is thick, stirring frequently to prevent sticking.

Increase the heat to high and stir-fry for at least 10 minutes, until the oil separates out from the coconut sauce. Continue stir-frying until the rendang is quite dry. Discard the bay leaf. Serve hot, sprinkled with desiccated coconut and garnished with bay leaves.

SERVES 4

Nutritional content per serving: Carbohydrate: 3   Fat: 28   Kilocalories: 350

Sizzling Steak with Mango; Beef Rendang (bottom); Sautéd Calves' Liver with Sherry and Sage

SAUTÉD CALVES' LIVER WITH SHERRY AND SAGE

THIS IS A SPECIAL DISH FOR 2 PEOPLE. IF YOU WANT TO BE LESS EXTRAVAGANT, REPLACE THE WINE WITH BEEF STOCK AND THE SHERRY WITH SHERRY VINEGAR

2 tablespoons dry sherry
2 tablespoons Worcestershire sauce
1 teaspoon chopped fresh sage or ½ teaspoon
   dried sage
2 slices calves' liver, total weight 175-250 g
   (6-8 oz), cut into thin strips
2 tablespoons olive oil
1 Spanish onion, sliced thinly
2 teaspoons plain flour
75 ml (3 fl oz) dry white wine
salt and pepper
fresh sage leaves to garnish

Whisk the sherry in a shallow dish with the Worcestershire sauce and sage. Add the strips of calves' liver and turn to coat. Cover and leave to marinate for about 20 minutes, turning the liver occasionally.

Heat the wok until hot. Add the oil and heat over a moderate heat until hot but not smoking. Add the onion slices and stir-fry for 5 minutes until softened. Remove with a slotted spoon and set aside.

Add the strips of liver and stir-fry over a moderate heat for 1-2 minutes until browned on all sides. Remove with a slotted spoon and set aside.

Sprinkle the flour into the wok and stir-fry until golden brown. Gradually stir in the wine and any marinade from the liver. Bring to the boil over a high heat, stirring constantly, then lower the heat, return the liver to the wok and simmer for a further 2-3 minutes until tender.

Add the onions and salt and pepper to taste, increase the heat to high and toss to combine. Serve at once, sprinkled with fresh sage leaves.

SERVES 2

Nutritional content per serving: Carbohydrate: 12   Fat: 25   Fibre: 2   Kilocalories: 445

STIR-FRIED BEEF WITH CRUNCHY VEGETABLES

MIXING YELLOW BEAN SAUCE WITH BEEF AND A COLOURFUL COLLECTION OF VEGETABLES IS AN EXCEPTIONALLY QUICK AND EASY WAY TO MAKE AN AUTHENTIC CHINESE DISH

250 g (8 oz) rump steak
2 tablespoons groundnut or vegetable oil
2 cloves garlic, crushed
1 large carrot, sliced thinly on the diagonal
250 g (8 oz) green or white cauliflower, florets
    separated, stalks sliced thinly on the
    diagonal
125 g (4 oz) green beans, sliced diagonally
    into 4 cm (1½ inch) lengths
½ × 160 g (5½ oz) jar yellow bean sauce
4 tablespoons water
1 tablespoon soy sauce
125 g (4 oz) bean sprouts
salt

Wrap the steak and place in the freezer for about 1 hour or until just frozen, then cut into thin strips across the grain, discarding any fat and sinew.

Heat the wok until hot. Add the oil and heat over a moderate heat until hot. Add the meat and garlic, increase the heat to high and stir-fry for about 2 minutes or until the meat is browned on all sides. Remove with a slotted spoon and set aside on a plate.

Add the carrot, cauliflower and beans and stir-fry for 3-4 minutes. Add the yellow bean sauce, water and soy sauce and stir-fry until well mixed.

Return the meat and juices to the wok, add the bean sprouts and stir-fry for a further 2 minutes or until the flavours are blended and the mixture is hot. Add salt to taste, if necessary. Serve at once.

SERVES 2-3

Nutritional content per serving: Carbohydrate: 18   Fat: 33   Fibre: 12   Kilocalories: 495

MA PO'S MINCED BEEF

THIS DISH IS NAMED AFTER THE LADY WHO INVENTED IT, WHO EARNED HERSELF THE NICKNAME 'MA PO' AFTER THE POCKMARKS ON HER FACE. TOFU (BEAN CURD) IS A HIGHLY NUTRITIOUS FOOD, OFTEN USED IN ORIENTAL COOKING AS A FORM OF INEXPENSIVE PROTEIN. IN THIS RECIPE IT MAKES A LITTLE MEAT GO A LONG WAY

2 teaspoons cornflour
150 ml (¼ pint) water
2 tablespoons soy sauce
2 tablespoons hoisin sauce
2 teaspoons chilli sauce
1 teaspoon soft dark brown sugar
3 tablespoons groundnut or vegetable oil
125 g (4 oz) minced beef
2 teaspoons black bean sauce
6 medium flat mushrooms, peeled and
    quartered
4 spring onions, sliced thinly into rounds
3 cloves garlic, crushed
1 × 297 g (10.5 oz) packet tofu (bean curd),
    drained, dried and diced
1 tablespoon sesame oil

Blend the cornflour in a jug with 3 tablespoons of the water, then add the remaining water, the soy, hoisin and chilli sauces and the sugar. Stir well to combine.

Heat the wok until hot. Add the oil and heat over a moderate heat until hot. Add the meat and black bean sauce, the mushrooms and half of the spring onions. Increase the heat to high and stir-fry for 3-4 minutes. Add the garlic, cornflour mixture and tofu (bean curd) and . bring to the boil, stirring constantly until thickened and glossy. Stir-fry for a further 2 minutes, then sprinkle over the remaining spring onions and the sesame oil. Serve at once.

SERVES 4

Nutritional content per serving: Carbohydrate: 9   Fat: 26   Fibre: 2   Kilocalories: 310

Bulgogi; Stir-Fried Beef with Crunchy Vegetables (top); Ma Po's Minced Beef

BULGOGI

BULGOGI IS ONE OF KOREA'S GREAT NATIONAL DISHES. TRADITIONALLY IT IS COOKED IN A CHARCOAL BURNER AT THE TABLE

500 g (1 lb) fillet steak
1 small Granny Smith apple, peeled, cored and grated
1 Conference pear, peeled, cored and grated
1 small onion, chopped finely
2 cloves garlic, chopped finely
4 tablespoons soy sauce
2 tablespoons wine vinegar
2 tablespoons soft dark brown sugar
2 teaspoons sesame seeds
2 tablespoons sesame oil
pepper
lemon balm or parsley sprigs to garnish

Wrap the steak and place in the freezer for about 1 hour, or until just frozen, then slice across the grain and cut into 4 cm (1 ½ inch) squares, discarding any fat and sinew.

Place the apple, pear, onion and garlic in a bowl with the soy sauce, vinegar, sugar and plenty of pepper. Add the squares of steak and stir well to mix. Cover and leave to marinate in the refrigerator for 24 hours, turning the meat occasionally.

When ready to cook, allow the meat to come to room temperature for about 1 hour. Meanwhile, put the sesame seeds in the wok and dry-fry over a moderate heat for 1-2 minutes until toasted. Remove from the wok and set aside.

Add the oil to the wok and heat over a moderate heat until hot but not smoking. Add the meat and marinade, increase the heat to high and stir-fry for 2 minutes or until the meat is browned on all sides. Garnish with lemon balm or parsley sprigs and serve at once, sprinkled with the toasted sesame seeds.

SERVES 4

Nutritional content per serving: Carbohydrate: 20   Fat: 38   Fibre: 2   Kilocalories: 515

PEPPER BEEF WITH MANGETOUT

SZECHUAN PEPPER IS A CHINESE FLAVOURING INGREDIENT FROM THE CITRUS FAMILY. IT IS A RED-BROWN COLOUR AND TASTES SHARP AND TANGY, RATHER THAN HOT LIKE BLACK PEPPER. IF YOU WOULD LIKE A HOT FLAVOUR TO THIS DISH, INCLUDE SOME – OR ALL – OF THE SEEDS FROM THE FRESH CHILLI

500 g (1 lb) fillet steak
2 tablespoons groundnut or vegetable oil
1 fresh green chilli, chopped finely, seeds
   discarded according to taste
2.5 cm (1 inch) piece fresh root ginger, peeled
   and chopped finely
4 spring onions, chopped finely
1 large red pepper, cored, deseeded and diced
250 g (8 oz) mangetout
1 tablespoon Szechuan pepper
1 tablespoon cornflour
4 tablespoons water
4 tablespoons soy sauce
2 tablespoons soft dark brown sugar

Wrap the steak and place in the freezer for about 1 hour, or until just frozen, then cut into thin slices across the grain.

Heat the wok until hot. Add 1 tablespoon oil and heat over a moderate heat until hot. Add the chilli, ginger, spring onions and red pepper and stir-fry over a gentle heat for 5 minutes until slightly softened. Add the mangetout, increase the heat to high and stir-fry for 2 minutes. Remove all of the vegetables with a slotted spoon and set aside on a plate.

Add the Szechuan pepper to the wok and dry-fry over a gentle heat for 1-2 minutes. Transfer to a mortar and crush with a pestle or the end of a straight wooden rolling pin.

Heat the remaining oil in the wok, add the meat and crushed pepper and increase the heat to high. Stir-fry for 2 minutes or until the meat is browned on all sides. Remove with a slotted spoon and set aside with the vegetables.

Blend the cornflour in a measuring jug with 2 tablespoons of the water, then add the remaining water, the soy sauce and sugar. Stir well to combine and make up to 300 ml (½ pint) with boiling water. Pour into the wok and bring to the boil over a high heat, stirring constantly until thickened and glossy. Return all the ingredients to the wok and stir-fry for about 1 minute or until heated through. Serve at once.

SERVES 4

Nutritional content per serving: Carbohydrate: 17   Fat: 37   Fibre: 3   Kilocalories: 500

Pepper Beef with Mangetout; Thai Beef Curry

THAI BEEF CURRY

500 g (1 lb) lean quick grill steaks
1 × 200 g (7 oz) packet creamed coconut
500 ml (17 fl oz) boiling water
2 medium red onions, sliced thinly
2 cloves garlic, crushed
5 cm (2 inch) piece fresh root ginger, peeled
  and chopped finely
2 dried red chillies, chopped roughly
roughly chopped rind and juice of
  1 lime
50 g (2 oz) shelled unsalted peanuts
2 teaspoons coriander seeds
seeds of 6 cardamom pods
2 tablespoons groundnut or vegetable oil
4 tablespoons chopped fresh coriander
2 teaspoons anchovy extract
1 teaspoon turmeric
½ teaspoon salt
500 g (1 lb) new potatoes, scraped and cut
  into bite-sized chunks
TO GARNISH:
coriander sprigs
lime wedges

Wrap the steaks and place in the freezer for about 1 hour or until just frozen, then cut into thin strips across the grain.

Dissolve one-quarter of the creamed coconut in 50 ml (2 fl oz) boiling water to make a thick coconut cream. Set aside. Dissolve the remaining coconut in the remaining boiling water to make a thin coconut milk.

Put the onions in a food processor or blender with the garlic, ginger, chillies, lime rind, peanuts, coriander and cardamom seeds. Add a few spoonfuls of the thin coconut milk and work to a paste.

Heat the wok until hot. Add the oil and heat over a moderate heat until hot. Add the meat, increase the heat to high and stir-fry for 1-2 minutes until the meat is browned on all sides. Add the paste, remaining thin coconut milk, the lime juice, half of the fresh coriander, the anchovy extract, turmeric and salt. Bring to the boil, stirring constantly.

Add the new potatoes. Lower the heat to a gentle simmer, then cover the wok. Cook for about 15 minutes, or until the meat and potatoes are tender, stirring frequently to prevent sticking. Serve hot, drizzled with the coconut cream and sprinkled with the remaining chopped coriander. Garnish with coriander sprigs and lime wedges.

SERVES 4

Nutritional content per serving: Carbohydrate: 31   Fat: 60   Fibre: 4   Kilocalories: 760

Bang bang beef

This recipe is based on the popular Chinese starter 'Bang Bang Chicken'. Here an inexpensive small joint of silverside is used, but you could use a thick slice of top rump or rump, or even fillet steak, depending on your budget

1 small red onion, chopped roughly
2 fresh green chillies, chopped roughly, seeds discarded according to taste
3 cloves garlic, chopped roughly
2 tablespoons coriander seeds
1 teaspoon cumin seeds
1 tablespoon groundnut or vegetable oil
1 × 750 g (1½ lb) joint silverside of beef, trimmed of fat
250 ml (8 fl oz) beef stock
2 tablespoons dry sherry or sherry vinegar
1 tablespoon soft dark brown sugar
spring onions to garnish

Pound the onion and chillies in a pestle and mortar with the garlic, coriander and cumin seeds or alternatively use the end of a straight wooden rolling pin.

Heat the wok until hot. Add the oil and heat over a moderate heat until hot. Add the meat and fry quickly until browned on all sides. Remove from the wok and set aside.

Add the pounded mixture and stir-fry over a gentle heat for 2-3 minutes, to blend the flavours without browning the ingredients. Pour in the stock, add the sherry or vinegar and sugar and bring to the boil, stirring.

Lower the heat, add the meat and cover the wok. Simmer for about 2 hours or until the meat is tender, turning the joint over and basting with the stock every 30 minutes. Remove the meat from the wok, cover and allow to cool then place in the refrigerator to chill for at least 2 hours or overnight.

Strain the sauce and, if you like, boil in a clean pan until thickened. Pour the sauce into a jug and chill with the meat.

Garnish with spring onions and serve the cold meat thinly sliced as a starter with a little of the sauce drizzled over. A salad of shredded carrots, white cabbage, spring onions and bean sprouts tossed in an oil, vinegar and soy dressing would make a good accompaniment.

SERVES 4

Nutritional content per serving: Carbohydrate: 6   Fat: 13   Kilocalories: 390

Bang Bang Beef; Stir-Fried Beef with Cashews

STIR-FRIED BEEF WITH CASHEWS

375 g (12 oz) flash-fry steak
4 tablespoons walnut oil
1 clove garlic, crushed
5 tablespoons teriyaki marinade
1 × 100 g (3.53 oz) packet unsalted cashew
  kernels
125 g (4 oz) mangetout
1 large green or red pepper, cored, deseeded
  and cut lengthways into thin strips
4 spring onions, sliced diagonally into 4 cm
  (1½ inch) lengths
salt and pepper

Wrap the steak and place in the freezer for about 1 hour, or until just frozen, then cut into thin slices.

Heat the wok until hot. Add 2 tablespoons oil and heat over a moderate heat until hot but not smoking. Add the meat, increase the heat to high and stir-fry for 2-3 minutes until the meat is browned on all sides. Transfer the meat to a bowl with a slotted spoon; add the garlic and 3 tablespoons teriyaki marinade and stir well to mix. Leave to cool.

Add 1 tablespoon oil to the wok and heat as before. Add the cashews and stir-fry for 1-2 minutes until golden brown, then remove from the oil with a slotted spoon and drain on kitchen paper.

Heat the remaining oil in the wok. Add the vegetables, increase the heat to high and stir-fry for 2 minutes. Add the meat mixture and the remaining teriyaki marinade to the wok and stir-fry for 30 seconds. Throw in the cashews and stir-fry for a further 30 seconds or until all the ingredients are heated through and evenly mixed. Season to taste and serve at once.

SERVES 4

Nutritional content per serving: Carbohydrate: 10   Fat: 39   Fibre: 4   Kilocalories: 475

PEKING BEEF

375 g (12 oz) rump steak
1 egg white
2 teaspoons cornflour
1 teaspoon mustard powder
½ teaspoon Chinese five-spice powder
2 tablespoons groundnut or vegetable oil
6 celery sticks, sliced thinly on the diagonal
SAUCE:
2 teaspoons cornflour
6 tablespoons water
2 tablespoons soy sauce
1 tablespoon red or white wine vinegar
1 tablespoon soft dark or light brown sugar
1 tablespoon tomato purée
2 teaspoons mustard powder
¼ teaspoon salt

Wrap the steak and place in the freezer for about 1 hour, or until just frozen, then cut into thin strips across the grain, discarding any fat.

Lightly beat the egg white in a shallow dish with the cornflour, mustard and five-spice powder. Add the strips of steak and turn to coat. Set aside.

Prepare the sauce: blend the cornflour in a jug with 2 tablespoons of the water, then add the remaining water and the remaining sauce ingredients. Stir well to combine.

Heat the wok until hot. Add 1 tablespoon oil and heat over a moderate heat until hot. Add the celery and stir-fry for 2 minutes, then remove with a slotted spoon and set aside.

Heat the remaining oil in the wok. Add about one-quarter of the meat, increase the heat to high and stir-fry for 2-3 minutes until browned on all sides. Remove with a slotted spoon and set aside on a plate. Repeat with the remaining meat, stir-frying it in batches.

Pour the sauce mixture into the wok and bring to the boil over a high heat, stirring constantly until thickened and glossy. Return the meat and any juices and the celery to the wok and stir-fry for about 30 seconds or until coated in the sauce. Serve at once.

SERVES 4

Nutritional content per serving: Carbohydrate: 9   Fat: 13   Fibre: 1   Kilocalories: 230

Peking Beef; Szechuan Shredded Beef

SZECHUAN SHREDDED BEEF

SZECHUAN DISHES COME FROM THE WESTERN REGION OF CHINA, AND ARE CHARACTERIZED BY RICH, SPICY FLAVOURS AND THE FREQUENT INCLUSION OF CHILLIES. THE SEEDS OF CHILLIES ARE THE HOTTEST PART, SO INCLUDE AS FEW – OR AS MANY – AS YOU LIKE

250 g (8 oz) rump or flash-fry steak
1 tablespoon Szechuan pepper
2 tablespoons soy sauce
1 tablespoon dry sherry or sherry vinegar
1 tablespoon hoisin sauce
1 tablespoon soft dark brown sugar
½ teaspoon Chinese five-spice powder
2 tablespoons groundnut or vegetable oil
2 fresh green chillies, sliced thinly, seeds discarded if liked
1 × 425 g (15 oz) can baby sweetcorn cobs, drained or 250 g (8 oz) fresh baby sweetcorn cobs
1 × 280 g (9 oz) can bean sprouts, drained or 175 g (6 oz) fresh bean sprouts
1 × 227 g (8 oz) can sliced bamboo shoots, drained

Wrap the steak and place in the freezer for about 1 hour, or until just frozen, then cut into thin strips (across the grain if using rump steak, and discarding any fat and sinew).

Crush the Szechuan pepper in a pestle and mortar or with the end of a straight wooden rolling pin, then mix in a jug with the remaining ingredients except the oil, chillies and vegetables.

Heat the wok until hot. Add the oil and heat over a moderate heat until hot. Add the meat, increase the heat to high and stir-fry for 2-3 minutes until browned on all sides. Add the chillies and stir-fry for a few seconds.

If using fresh sweetcorn blanch in boiling salted water for 3-4 minutes before using. Add all of the vegetables to the wok, then the Szechuan pepper mixture. Stir-fry for 2-3 minutes or until the flavours are blended and the vegetables are hot. Serve at once.

SERVES 3-4

Nutritional content per serving: Carbohydrate: 15   Fat: 23   Fibre: 2   Kilocalories: 355

Poultry

CHICKEN, DUCK AND TURKEY ARE THE PERFECT MEATS FOR STIR-FRYING. THEY REQUIRE VERY LITTLE PREPARATION AND BECOME TENDER IN MOMENTS. ALL THREE MEATS ARE INTERCHANGEABLE IN THE RECIPES IN THIS CHAPTER, SO YOU CAN RING THE CHANGES WITH THEIR DIFFERENT FLAVOURS.

CHICKEN WITH CASHEW NUTS

1 teaspoon cornflour

4 tablespoons cold chicken stock or water

2 tablespoons hoisin sauce

2 tablespoons dry sherry or sherry vinegar

1 teaspoon soft dark brown sugar

2 tablespoons groundnut or vegetable oil

375 g (12 oz) chicken breast fillets, cut into thin strips

½ bunch spring onions, sliced diagonally into 2.5 cm (1 inch) lengths

1 × 100 g (3.53 oz) packet unsalted cashew kernels

2 cloves garlic, chopped finely

salt and pepper

Blend the cornflour in a jug with 1 tablespoon of the stock or water, then add the remaining stock or water, the hoisin sauce, sherry or vinegar and sugar. Stir well to combine.

Heat the wok until hot. Add the oil and heat over a moderate heat until hot. Add the chicken, increase the heat to high and stir-fry for 2-3 minutes, then add the spring onions, cashews and garlic. Stir-fry for 30 seconds, or until all of the ingredients are combined, then pour in the cornflour mixture and bring to the boil over a high heat, stirring constantly until thickened and glossy. Stir-fry for 2 minutes or until the chicken is tender and evenly coated in the sauce. Add salt and pepper to taste. Serve at once.

SERVES 3-4

Nutritional content per serving: Carbohydrate: 12   Fat: 29   Fibre: 2   Kilocalories: 445

LEMON CHICKEN

THIS SIMPLE RECIPE ORIGINATED IN HONG KONG. IT IS DELICIOUS SERVED WITH SPINACH OR BROCCOLI

1 egg white

2 teaspoons cornflour

pinch of salt

250 g (8 oz) chicken breast fillets, cut into thin strips

vegetable oil for shallow frying

lemon balm sprigs or lemon slices to garnish

SAUCE:

2 teaspoons cornflour

6 tablespoons cold chicken stock or water

finely grated rind of ½ lemon

2 tablespoons lemon juice

1 tablespoon soy sauce

2 teaspoons dry sherry or sherry vinegar

2 teaspoons caster sugar

Lightly beat the egg white in a shallow dish with the cornflour and salt. Add the strips of chicken and turn gently to coat. Set aside.

Prepare the sauce: blend the cornflour in a jug with 2 tablespoons of the stock or water, then add the remaining stock or water and the remaining sauce ingredients. Stir well to combine.

Pour enough oil into the wok to come 2.5-4 cm (1-1 ½ inches) up the sides. Heat over a moderate heat until hot but not smoking, then shallow fry a few strips of chicken for about 2 minutes or until lightly browned. Lift out with a slotted spoon and drain on kitchen paper while shallow frying the remainder.

Carefully pour the oil out of the wok. Pour in the sauce mixture and bring to the boil over a high heat, stirring constantly until thickened and glossy. Return the chicken to the wok and stir-fry for 2 minutes or until tender and evenly coated in the lemon sauce. Garnish with lemon balm or lemon slices and serve at once.

SERVES 2

Nutritional content per serving: Carbohydrate: 11   Fat: 35   Kilocalories: 475

Lemon Chicken; Chicken with Cashew Nuts

DUCK WITH ORANGE AND BEAN SPROUTS

pared rind of ½ orange
1 tablespoon cornflour
6 tablespoons water
1 tablespoon dry sherry or sherry vinegar
1 tablespoon orange juice
1 tablespoon soy sauce
2 teaspoons hoisin sauce
1 teaspoon soft dark brown sugar
seeds of 6 cardamom pods, crushed
2 tablespoons groundnut or vegetable oil
1 clove garlic, crushed
2.5 cm (1 inch) piece fresh root ginger,
   peeled and cut into thin strips
375 g (12 oz) duckling breast fillets, skin
   and fat removed, cut into thin strips
250 g (8 oz) bean sprouts
segments of 1 orange

Cut the orange rind into matchstick strips, blanch in boiling water for 1 minute, then drain, rinse and pat dry.

Blend the cornflour in a jug with 2 tablespoons of the water, then add the remaining water, the sherry or vinegar, orange juice, soy and hoisin sauces, sugar and cardamom seeds. Stir well to combine.

Heat the wok until hot. Add the oil and heat over a moderate heat until hot. Add the garlic and ginger and stir-fry for a few seconds. Add the duckling, increase the heat to high and stir-fry for 3-4 minutes. Pour in the cornflour mixture and bring to the boil over a high heat, stirring constantly until thickened and glossy. Stir-fry for 3 more minutes, then add the bean sprouts and orange rind and stir-fry for 1 minute or until the duckling is tender. Add the orange segments and heat through for 30 seconds. Serve at once.

SERVES 2-3

Nutritional content per serving: Carbohydrate: 18   Fat: 23   Fibre: 2   Kilocalories: 420

QUICK-FRIED CHICKEN WITH MUSHROOMS AND PEAS

250 g (8 oz) long-grain rice
125 g (4 oz) frozen petits pois
1 tablespoon cornflour
6 tablespoons cold chicken stock or water
2 tablespoons lemon juice
2 tablespoons groundnut or vegetable oil
2 spring onions, cut into thin rings
2 celery sticks, chopped finely
4 chicken breast fillets, cut into thin strips
4 rashers smoked bacon, derinded and diced
175 g (6 oz) button mushrooms, sliced thinly
½ teaspoon dried mint
salt and pepper
mint leaves to garnish

Cook the rice in boiling salted water according to packet instructions, gently folding in the frozen petits pois for the last 5 minutes of the cooking time.

Blend the cornflour in a jug with 2 tablespoons of the stock or water, then add the remaining stock or water and the lemon juice. Stir well to combine.

Heat the wok until hot. Add the oil and heat over a moderate heat until hot. Add the spring onions and celery and stir-fry over a gentle heat for 1-2 minutes until slightly softened. Add the chicken and bacon, increase the heat to high and stir-fry for 2-3 minutes.

Add the rice and peas and the mushrooms and toss to combine with the chicken mixture. Pour in the cornflour mixture and bring to the boil over a high heat, stirring constantly until thickened. Stir-fry for 2 more minutes until the chicken is tender and all the ingredients are evenly combined. Add the mint and salt and pepper to taste and garnish with mint leaves. Serve at once.

SERVES 4

Nutritional content per serving: Carbohydrate: 56   Fat: 11   Fibre: 6   Kilocalories: 390

Duck with Orange and Bean Sprouts; Quick-Fried Chicken with Mushrooms and Peas (bottom); Chicken Malay

CHICKEN MALAY

IN MALAYSIA, THE AROMATIC HERB LEMON GRASS IS COMMONLY USED AS A FLAVOURING INGREDIENT. LEMON RIND IS USED AS A SUBSTITUTE FOR IT IN THIS RECIPE, TO EQUALLY GOOD EFFECT

4 chicken thighs, total weight about 500 g (1 lb), skinned and boned
2 boneless chicken breasts, weighing about 175 g (6 oz) each, halved lengthways
1 teaspoon turmeric
1 cm (½ inch) piece root ginger, peeled and chopped roughly
1 clove garlic, chopped roughly
1 fresh green chilli, chopped roughly, seeds discarded according to taste
75 g (3 oz) creamed coconut
300 ml (½ pint) boiling water
1 tablespoon groundnut or vegetable oil
2 bay leaves
seeds of 2 cardamom pods
strip of lemon rind
bay leaves to garnish

Slash the chicken flesh with a sharp knife, then rub in the turmeric.

Pound the ginger and garlic with the chilli in a pestle and mortar or with the end of a straight wooden rolling pin. Dissolve the creamed coconut in the boiling water to make coconut milk; set aside.

Heat the wok until hot. Add the oil and heat over a moderate heat until hot. Add the pounded mixture and stir-fry over a gentle heat for 2-3 minutes to blend the flavours without browning the ingredients.

Add the chicken thighs, increase the heat to high and stir-fry for 5 minutes. Add the chicken breasts and stir-fry for 1 minute. Add the coconut milk, bay leaves, cardamom seeds and lemon rind and bring to the boil, stirring. Lower the heat and simmer for 15 minutes, or until the chicken is tender and the sauce thickened, stirring frequently. Discard the bay leaves and lemon rind. Serve hot, garnished with fresh bay leaves.

SERVES 4

Nutritional content per serving: Carbohydrate: 56   Fat: 12   Kilocalories: 275

QUICK-FRIED RIBBONS OF DUCK WITH PLUM AND GINGER SAUCE

1 tablespoon groundnut or vegetable oil

375 g (12 oz) duckling breast fillets, skin and fat removed, cut into thin strips

250 g (8 oz) red plums, halved, stoned and cut into thin strips

4 tablespoons chicken stock or water

1 tablespoon hoisin sauce

2 teaspoons orange juice

2 teaspoons granulated sugar

1 teaspoon soy sauce

½ teaspoon ground ginger

¼ teaspoon Chinese five-spice powder

spring onion slices to garnish

Heat the wok until hot. Add the oil and heat over a moderate heat until hot. Add the duckling, increase the heat to high and stir-fry for 4-5 minutes. Remove the duckling with a slotted spoon and set aside.

Add the plums to the wok with the stock or water, hoisin sauce, orange juice, sugar, soy sauce, ginger and five-spice powder. Stir-fry to mix, then lower the heat and simmer for about 10 minutes, or until the plums are soft.

Return the duckling to the wok, increase the heat to high and boil rapidly until the duckling is tender and glazed with the sauce. Serve at once, garnished with spring onion slices.

SERVES 2-3

Nutritional content per serving: Carbohydrate: 14   Fat: 17   Fibre: 3   Kilocalories: 355

SINGAPOREAN ALMOND CHICKEN

1 red onion, sliced thinly

1 tablespoon soy sauce

1 tablespoon dry sherry or sherry vinegar

1 teaspoon sesame oil

½ teaspoon Chinese five-spice powder

375 g (12 oz) chicken thighs, boned, skinned and cut into 1 cm (½ inch) pieces

1 × 20 g (1 oz) drum dried sliced mushrooms

2 teaspoons cornflour

8 tablespoons cold chicken stock or water

1 teaspoon tomato purée

125 ml (4 fl oz) vegetable oil for shallow frying

50 g (2 oz) whole blanched almonds

125 g (4 oz) lean sliced cooked ham, cut into thin strips

1 × 227 g (8 oz) can sliced bamboo shoots, drained

Whisk the onion in a bowl with the soy sauce, sherry or vinegar, sesame oil and five-spice powder. Add the pieces of chicken and stir well to mix. Cover and leave to marinate for 20-30 minutes, turning the chicken occasionally.

Meanwhile, cook the dried mushrooms in boiling water for 10 minutes, according to the instructions on the drum. Drain. Blend the cornflour in a jug with 2 tablespoons of the stock or water, then add the remaining stock or water and the tomato purée. Stir well to combine.

Heat the vegetable oil in the wok until hot. Add the almonds and shallow fry until golden brown. Lift out with a slotted spoon and drain on kitchen paper.

Carefully pour all but 1 tablespoon of oil out of the wok. Add the chicken and marinade and stir-fry over a high heat for 2-3 minutes. Pour in the cornflour mixture and bring to the boil over a high heat, stirring constantly until thickened and glossy. Add the mushrooms with the ham and bamboo shoots. Stir-fry for 1-2 minutes until the chicken is tender and all the ingredients are evenly combined. Serve at once, topped with the fried almonds.

SERVES 4

Nutritional content per serving: Carbohydrate: 7   Fat: 45   Fibre: 2   Kilocalories: 535

Quick-Fried Ribbons of Duck with Plum and Ginger Sauce; Singaporean Almond Chicken; Orange Chicken

ORANGE CHICKEN

THIS RECIPE IS MALAYSIAN. NOT ONLY DOES IT TASTE SWEET AND DELICIOUS, IT LOOKS VERY PRETTY TOO

4 chicken breast fillets, skinned

2 egg whites

2 tablespoons plain flour

4 teaspoons cornflour

175 ml (6 fl oz) freshly squeezed orange juice

4 tablespoons orange squash

2 teaspoons sesame oil

vegetable oil, for deep frying

125 g (4 oz) frozen petits pois

1 bunch spring onions, sliced diagonally into
   4 cm (1½ inch) lengths

salt

orange slices to garnish

Cut each chicken breast crossways on the diagonal into 6-8 slices. Lightly beat the egg whites in a shallow dish with the flour and ¼ teaspoon salt. Add the slices of chicken and turn to coat. Set aside.

Blend the cornflour in a jug with 2 tablespoons of the orange juice, then add the remaining orange juice, the orange squash, sesame oil and salt to taste. Stir well to combine.

Pour enough oil into the wok for deep frying and heat to 190°C, 375°F or until a cube of bread browns in 30 seconds. Deep fry a few slices of chicken for about 3-4 minutes until tender and golden. Lift out with a slotted spoon and drain on kitchen paper while deep frying the remainder. When all the chicken has been drained, transfer the slices to a warmed serving dish and keep hot.

Carefully pour all but 2 tablespoons of oil out of the wok. Add the frozen peas and half of the spring onions and stir-fry over a moderate heat for 2-3 minutes. Pour in the cornflour mixture and bring to the boil over a high heat, stirring constantly until thickened and glossy. Taste the sauce and add more salt if necessary, then pour over the chicken. Serve at once, garnished with the remaining spring onions and the orange slices.

SERVES 4

Nutritional content per serving: Carbohydrate: 20   Fat: 18   Fibre: 3   Kilocalories: 350

SHANGHAI STIR-FRY

SHANGHAI, IN THE EAST OF CHINA, IS NOTED FOR ITS RICH AND EXQUISITELY PRESENTED CUISINE. MANY DISHES LIKE THIS ONE INCLUDE SUGAR AMONGST THEIR INGREDIENTS, GIVING THE CHARACTERISTIC SWEET TASTE OF THE REGION

2 teaspoons cornflour
6 tablespoons cold chicken stock or water
3 tablespoons soy sauce
2 tablespoons dry sherry or sherry vinegar
1½ tablespoons soft dark brown sugar
2 tablespoons groundnut or vegetable oil
40 g (1½ oz) pine kernels
4 chicken breast fillets, cut into thin strips
1 large red pepper, cored, deseeded and cut
   lengthways into thin strips
250 g (8 oz) white cabbage or Chinese leaves,
   shredded
4 spring onions, chopped finely
2.5 cm (1 inch) piece fresh root ginger, peeled
   and chopped finely
250 g (8 oz) bean sprouts
1-2 teaspoons sesame oil

Blend the cornflour in a jug with 1 tablespoon of the stock or water, then add the remaining stock or water, the soy sauce, sherry or vinegar and sugar. Stir well to combine.

Heat the wok until hot. Add 1 tablespoon oil and heat over a moderate heat until hot. Add the pine kernels and stir-fry for 1-2 minutes until toasted. Remove with a slotted spoon and drain on kitchen paper. Heat the remaining oil in the wok. Add the chicken, increase the heat to high and stir-fry for 2-3 minutes. Remove with a slotted spoon and set aside. Add the red pepper to the wok with the cabbage or Chinese leaves, spring onions, ginger and bean sprouts. Stir-fry for 2 minutes, then pour in the cornflour mixture and bring to the boil over a high heat, stirring constantly until thickened and glossy. Return the chicken to the wok and stir-fry for 2 minutes or until tender and evenly combined with the vegetables. Serve at once, sprinkled with the toasted pine kernels and sesame oil.

SERVES 4

Nutritional content per serving: Carbohydrate: 26   Fat: 19   Fibre: 4   Kilocalories: 400

HOT DICED CHICKEN WITH PEANUT SAUCE

THE FLAVOUR OF THIS SAUCE IS SIMILAR TO THAT OF INDONESIAN SATAY

½ × 200 g (7 oz) packet creamed coconut
300 ml (½ pint) boiling water
500 g (1 lb) chicken breast fillets, cut into
   thin strips
1 teaspoon chilli powder
3 tablespoons groundnut or vegetable oil
2 tablespoons crunchy peanut butter
2 tablespoons chilli sauce
1 teaspoon soft dark brown sugar
¼ teaspoon salt
coriander sprigs to garnish

Dissolve the creamed coconut in the boiling water to make coconut milk; set aside. Sprinkle the chicken with the chilli powder.

Heat the wok until hot. Add 2 tablespoons oil and heat over a moderate heat until hot. Add the chicken, increase the heat to high and stir-fry for 2-3 minutes. Remove the chicken with a slotted spoon and set aside.

Heat the remaining oil in the wok, add the peanut butter and chilli sauce and stir-fry to mix. Stir in the coconut milk a little at a time, bring to the boil, stirring constantly, then add the sugar and salt.

Return the chicken to the wok and continue stir-frying for 3-4 minutes until the chicken is tender and the oil separates out from the sauce. Garnish with coriander sprigs and serve at once.

SERVES 4

Nutritional content per serving: Carbohydrate: 5   Fat: 37   Fibre: 1   Kilocalories: 465

Shanghai Stir-Fry; Hot Diced Chicken with Peanut Sauce; Kung Pao Chicken

KUNG PAO CHICKEN

THIS FAMOUS DISH IS SAID TO HAVE BEEN A FAVOURITE OF THE SZECHUAN GOVERNOR KUNG PAO

1 egg white

2 teaspoons cornflour

2 teaspoons soy sauce

2 teaspoons dry sherry or sherry vinegar

500 g (1 lb) chicken breast fillets, cut into bite-sized cubes

2 tablespoons groundnut or vegetable oil

1 large red pepper, cored, deseeded and chopped finely

3 dried red chillies, crushed

3 cloves garlic, crushed

5 cm (2 inch) piece fresh root ginger, peeled and chopped finely

50 g (2 oz) shelled unsalted peanuts

SAUCE:

4 teaspoons cornflour

8 tablespoons chicken stock or water

2 tablespoons white wine vinegar

2 tablespoons soy sauce

1 tablespoon chilli sauce

1 tablespoon soft dark or light brown sugar

2 teaspoons tomato purée

Lightly beat the egg white in a shallow dish with the cornflour, soy sauce and sherry or vinegar. Add the cubes of chicken and turn to coat. Set aside.

Prepare the sauce: blend the cornflour in a jug with 2 tablespoons of the stock or water, then add the remaining stock or water and the remaining ingredients. Stir well to combine.

Heat the wok until hot. Add the oil and heat over a moderate heat until hot. Add the red pepper, chillies, garlic and ginger and stir-fry over a gentle heat for 2-3 minutes to blend the flavours without browning the ingredients.

Add about one-quarter of the chicken and marinade, increase the heat to high and stir-fry for 2-3 minutes. Remove with a slotted spoon and set aside. Repeat with the remaining chicken.

Pour the sauce mixture into the wok and bring to the boil over a high heat, stirring constantly until thickened and glossy. Return all the chicken to the wok and stir-fry for 2 more minutes, or until the chicken is tender and evenly coated in the sauce. Stir in the peanuts and serve at once.

SERVES 4

Nutritional content per serving: Carbohydrate: 17   Fat: 19   Fibre: 2   Kilocalories: 365

CHILLI CHICKEN

CHAIRMAN MAO WAS SAID TO HAVE BEEN VERY FOND OF DEEP-FRIED CHICKEN SERVED WITH HOT CHILLI SAUCE. HERE IS A VARIATION ON THE THEME

1 egg white
1 tablespoon cornflour
pinch of salt
500 g (1 lb) chicken breast fillets, cut into thin strips
vegetable oil, for deep frying
1 cm (½ inch) piece fresh root ginger, peeled and chopped finely
2 cloves garlic, crushed
250 g (8 oz) carrots, sliced thinly on the diagonal
1 red or green pepper, cored, deseeded and cut into 1 cm (½ inch) squares
3 spring onions, chopped finely
50 g (2 oz) canned sliced bamboo shoots, drained
2 spring onions, sliced thinly on the diagonal, to garnish
SAUCE:
2 teaspoons cornflour
4 tablespoons chicken stock or water
2 tablespoons chilli sauce
1 tablespoon soy sauce
1 tablespoon dry sherry or sherry vinegar
1 teaspoon soft dark brown sugar

Lightly beat the egg white in a shallow dish with the cornflour and salt. Add the strips of chicken and turn to coat. Set aside.

Prepare the sauce: blend the cornflour in a jug with 1 tablespoon of the stock or water, then add the remaining stock or water and the remaining sauce ingredients. Stir well to combine.

Pour enough oil into the wok for deep frying and heat to 190°C, 375°F or until a cube of bread browns in 30 seconds. Deep fry a few strips of chicken in the oil for 2-3 minutes until golden and crisp. Lift out with a slotted spoon and drain on kitchen paper while deep frying the remainder.

Carefully pour all but 1 tablespoon of oil out of the wok. Add the ginger and garlic and stir-fry over a gentle heat for a few seconds, to flavour the oil. Add the carrots, pepper and spring onions and stir-fry for 2 minutes, or until the carrots are tender-crisp. Pour in the sauce mixture and bring to the boil, stirring constantly until thickened and glossy. Add the chicken and bamboo shoots and stir-fry for 1 minute or until the chicken is tender and coated in the sauce.

Sprinkle with the spring onion to garnish and serve at once.

SERVES 4

Nutritional content per serving:	Carbohydrate: 13	Fat: 20	Fibre: 3	Kilocalories: 350

Chilli Chicken; Rapid-Fried Chicken Livers with Mangetout

RAPID-FRIED CHICKEN LIVERS WITH MANGETOUT

TO OFFSET THE RICHNESS OF THIS PIQUANT SUPPER DISH, SERVE WITH PLAIN BOILED NUTTY BROWN RICE AND A REFRESHINGLY COOL CUCUMBER OR MIXED GREEN SALAD

1 tablespoon cornflour

8 tablespoons cold chicken stock or water

1 tablespoon tomato purée or ketchup

1 tablespoon dry sherry or sherry vinegar

2 teaspoons Worcestershire sauce

1 teaspoon lemon juice

2 tablespoons groundnut or vegetable oil

250 g (8 oz) mangetout, cut in half crossways
  if large

1 small onion, sliced finely

1 × 227 g (8 oz) tub frozen chicken livers,
  defrosted, dried, and cut into 2.5 cm
  (1 inch) thick slices

1 clove garlic, crushed

pepper

parsley sprigs to garnish

Blend the cornflour in a jug with 2 tablespoons of the stock or water, then add the remaining stock or water, the tomato purée or ketchup, sherry or vinegar, Worcestershire sauce and lemon juice. Stir well to combine.

Heat the wok until hot. Add 1 tablespoon oil and heat over a moderate heat until hot. Add the mangetout, increase the heat to high and stir-fry for 2 minutes. Remove with a slotted spoon and set aside.

Heat the remaining oil in the wok over a moderate heat. Add the onion and stir-fry for 2 minutes. Add the chicken livers and garlic and stir-fry for 2-3 minutes until the chicken livers lose their pink colour. Pour in the cornflour mixture and bring to the boil over a high heat, stirring constantly until thickened and glossy. Lower the heat, add plenty of pepper and simmer gently for 5 minutes or until the livers are cooked but still pink in the centre.

Return the mangetout to the wok, increase the heat and toss over a high heat until hot and evenly combined with the livers. Serve at once, garnished with parsley.

SERVES 3-4

Nutritional content per serving: Carbohydrate: 9   Fat: 15   Fibre: 3   Kilocalories: 240

CHICKEN WITH COCONUT AND LIME

4 chicken breast fillets
½ × 200 g (7 oz) packet creamed coconut
300 ml (½ pint) boiling water
1 tablespoon butter or margarine
1 tablespoon groundnut or vegetable oil
1 red onion, chopped finely
juice of ½ lime
MARINADE:
finely grated rind and juice of ½ lime
2.5 cm (1 inch) piece fresh root ginger, peeled and crushed
1 clove garlic, crushed
1 tablespoon soy sauce
2 teaspoons ground coriander
2 teaspoons soft light brown sugar
¼ teaspoon ground cardamom
pinch of salt
TO GARNISH:
lime slices
coriander leaves

Whisk the marinade ingredients together in a bowl, add the chicken breast fillets and stir well to mix. Cover and leave to marinate for 1-2 hours, turning the fillets occasionally.

Meanwhile, dissolve the creamed coconut in the boiling water to make coconut milk.

When ready to cook, lift the chicken out of the marinade and brush off the pieces of lime rind, ginger and garlic. Reserve with the marinade. Heat the wok until hot. Add the butter or margarine and oil and heat over a moderate heat until foaming. Add the chicken, 2 fillets at a time, and cook for 2-3 minutes on each side until lightly coloured. Lift out with a slotted spoon and set aside.

Add the onion to the wok and stir-fry for 2 minutes. Add the reserved marinade and half of the coconut milk and bring to the boil. Lower the heat, return the chicken to the wok and simmer for 12-15 minutes, or until tender. Lift the chicken out with a slotted spoon, arrange on a warmed serving platter and keep warm.

Pour the remaining coconut milk into the wok, then add the lime juice. Bring to the boil over a high heat and simmer for 3-5 minutes until thickened, stirring constantly. Pour over the chicken, garnish with lime and coriander and serve at once.

SERVES 4

Nutritional content per serving: Carbohydrate: 9   Fat: 31   Fibre: 1   Kilocalories: 430

SOY CHICKEN

500 g (1 lb) chicken thighs, boned, skinned and cut into 2.5 cm (1 inch) pieces
2 tablespoons groundnut or vegetable oil
celery leaves to garnish
MARINADE:
3 tablespoons soy sauce
2 tablespoons tomato ketchup or purée
3 tablespoons wine or sherry vinegar
2 tablespoons soft dark brown sugar
2 teaspoons Worcestershire sauce
1 clove garlic, crushed
1-2 teaspoons chilli powder, according to taste
1 teaspoon celery salt

Combine the marinade ingredients in a large bowl, add the pieces of chicken and turn to coat. Cover and leave to marinate in the refrigerator for 4 hours or overnight, turning the chicken occasionally.

When ready to cook, allow the chicken to come to room temperature for about 30 minutes.

Heat the wok until hot. Add the oil and heat over a moderate heat until hot. Add the chicken and marinade, increase the heat to high and stir-fry for 2-3 minutes until the chicken is browned on all sides. Lower the heat and simmer for 6-7 minutes until the chicken is tender and the sauce is reduced, stirring occasionally.

Garnish with celery leaves and serve hot.

SERVES 4

Nutritional content per serving: Carbohydrate: 13   Fat: 16   Kilocalories: 295

Chicken with Coconut and Lime; Soy Chicken (bottom); Stir-Fried Turkey with Pine Kernels and Peppers

STIR-FRIED TURKEY WITH PINE KERNELS AND PEPPERS

1 tablespoon cornflour

6 tablespoons cold chicken stock or water

2 tablespoons dry sherry or sherry vinegar

2 tablespoons soy sauce

1 tablespoon lemon juice

½ teaspoon ground ginger

2 tablespoons groundnut or vegetable oil

500 g (1 lb) turkey breast steaks, cut into thin strips

1 clove garlic, crushed

1 small onion, sliced finely

1 large yellow pepper, cored, deseeded and cut lengthways into thin strips

1 large red pepper, cored, deseeded and cut lengthways into thin strips

40 g (1½ oz) pine kernels

Blend the cornflour in a jug with 2 tablespoons of the stock or water, then add the remaining stock or water, the sherry or vinegar, soy sauce, lemon juice and ginger. Stir well to combine.

Heat the wok until hot. Add the oil and heat over a moderate heat until hot. Add the turkey and garlic, increase the heat to high and stir-fry for 3-4 minutes. Lift out with a slotted spoon and set aside.

Lower the heat, add the onion to the wok and stir-fry for 1 minute, then add the peppers and stir-fry for 2 minutes. Pour in the cornflour mixture and bring to the boil over a high heat, stirring constantly until thickened and glossy. Return the turkey to the wok and stir-fry for 2 minutes or until tender and evenly coated in the sauce. Stir in the pine kernels and serve at once.

SERVES 4

Nutritional content per serving: Carbohydrate: 9   Fat: 10   Fibre: 2   Kilocalories: 253

HOT THAI SALAD

A GARNISH OF RADISH FLOWERS LOOKS VERY PRETTY ON THIS SUBSTANTIAL MAIN-COURSE SALAD. TO MAKE A RADISH FLOWER, HOLD THE RADISH WITH THE STALK END DOWNWARDS AND CUT 5 SHALLOW PETAL SHAPES IN THE RED SKIN. PLACE IN ICED WATER UNTIL THE PETALS FAN OUT SLIGHTLY

2 chicken breast fillets
250 g (8 oz) pork fillet (tenderloin)
50 g (2 oz) Chinese rice noodles (mihun)
6 tablespoons groundnut or vegetable oil
1 bunch spring onions, sliced thinly on the diagonal
5 cm (2 inch) piece fresh root ginger, peeled and cut into matchsticks
250 g (8 oz) cooked peeled prawns, defrosted and dried thoroughly if frozen
1 bunch radishes, sliced thinly
½ cucumber, sliced thinly
2 tomatoes, sliced thinly
1 small head Little Gem lettuce, shredded
4-6 radish flowers to garnish (see above)
DRESSING:
2 small fresh green chillies, chopped roughly, seeds discarded according to taste
2 cloves garlic, chopped roughly
finely grated rind of 1 lime
juice of 3 limes
2 teaspoons anchovy extract
2 teaspoons soft dark brown sugar

Wrap the chicken and pork and place in the freezer for about 1 hour, or until just frozen.

Cook the rice noodles according to packet instructions. Drain, rinse under cold running water and set aside. Make the dressing: pound the chillies and garlic with the lime rind in a pestle and mortar or with the end of a straight wooden rolling pin, then transfer to a jug or bowl. Add the lime juice, anchovy extract and sugar and stir until the sugar has dissolved; set aside.

Cut the chicken and pork into thin strips on the diagonal. Heat the wok until hot. Add one-third of the oil and heat over a moderate heat until hot. Add about one-third of the spring onions and ginger and stir-fry over a gentle heat for 2-3 minutes to blend the flavours without browning the ingredients.

Add the chicken strips and stir-fry over a moderate heat for 2-3 minutes or until tender. Remove the chicken, spring onions and ginger with a slotted spoon and set aside.

Repeat this method of stir-frying with the pork and prawns, adding the remaining oil, spring onions and ginger in 2 equal batches. Set aside.

Quickly pour the dressing into the wok and bring to the boil, stirring. Remove from the heat.

In a large bowl, toss the chicken, pork and prawns with the prepared salad ingredients and noodles. Pour over the hot dressing and toss again until evenly mixed. Garnish with radish flowers and serve at once.

SERVES 4-6

Nutritional content per serving:	Carbohydrate: 16	Fat: 31	Fibre: 2	Kilocalories: 505

Hot Thai Salad; Turkey Chow Mein

TURKEY CHOW MEIN

CHOW MEIN WAS INVENTED BY CHINESE EMIGRANTS IN SAN FRANCISCO; IT IS A VERY GOOD WAY OF USING UP LEFTOVER COOKED MEAT, HAM AND POULTRY, ESPECIALLY AROUND CHRISTMASTIME. THE NOODLES ARE OFTEN DEEP FRIED FOR CHOW MEIN, BUT THIS RECIPE USES BOILED NOODLES, WHICH ARE A HEALTHIER ALTERNATIVE

1 × 250 g (8 oz) packet Chinese rice noodles (mihun)

2 tablespoons groundnut or vegetable oil

3-4 spring onions, sliced thinly

2.5 cm (1 inch) piece fresh root ginger, chopped finely

1 clove garlic, crushed

250 g (8 oz) skinned and boned cooked turkey, cut into thin strips

200 g (7 oz) Chinese leaves, shredded

200 g (7 oz) bean sprouts

125 g (4 oz) lean sliced cooked ham, cut into thin strips

1 × 277 g (8 oz) can sliced bamboo shoots, drained

salt and pepper

SAUCE:

2 teaspoons cornflour

8 tablespoons cold chicken stock or water

2 tablespoons soy sauce

2 teaspoons sesame oil

Cook the rice noodles according to packet instructions.

Prepare the sauce: blend the cornflour in a jug with 2 tablespoons of the stock or water, then add the remaining stock or water, the soy sauce and sesame oil. Stir well to combine.

Drain the noodles, rinse under cold running water and set aside. Heat the wok until hot. Add the oil and heat over a moderate heat until hot. Add the spring onions, ginger and garlic and stir-fry over a gentle heat for 2-3 minutes to blend the flavours without browning the ingredients. Add the turkey, increase the heat to high and stir-fry for 2-3 minutes. Add the Chinese leaves and bean sprouts and stir-fry for 1-2 minutes until tender-crisp, then add the ham and bamboo shoots and stir-fry to mix. Pour in the sauce mixture and bring to the boil over a high heat, stirring constantly until thickened and glossy. Fold in the drained noodles, toss over a high heat until hot, then add salt and pepper to taste. Serve at once.

SERVES 4

Nutritional content per serving: Carbohydrate: 52   Fat: 15   Fibre: 4   Kilocalories: 460

Lamb and pork

LAMB AND PORK ARE USED EXTENSIVELY IN ORIENTIAL COOKING, AND MANY OF THE CLASSIC RECIPES CALL FOR ONE OR THE OTHER OF THESE POPULAR MEATS. BOTH ARE ECONOMICAL ENOUGH TO USE FOR EVERYDAY MEALS, YET EASILY ADAPT TO MAKE SOMETHING SPECIAL WHEN ENTERTAINING.

Nasi goreng

THIS CLASSIC INDONESIAN SPECIALITY IS OFTEN SERVED GARNISHED WITH PRAWN CRACKERS AND DEEP-FRIED ONION RINGS. EXTRA SOY SAUCE IS USUALLY SERVED AT THE TABLE, FOR THOSE WHO LIKE A MORE PRONOUNCED FLAVOUR

250 g (8 oz) pork fillet (tenderloin)
375 g (12 oz) long-grain rice
2 eggs, beaten
1½ tablespoons groundnut or vegetable oil
1 fresh green chilli, chopped roughly, seeds discarded according to taste
½ small onion, chopped roughly
2 cloves garlic, chopped roughly
500 g (1 lb) peeled cooked prawns, defrosted and dried thoroughly if frozen
6 tablespoons soy sauce
2 tablespoons tomato ketchup
2 teaspoons anchovy extract
2 tablespoons sesame oil
salt and pepper
parsley sprigs to garnish

Wrap the pork and place in the freezer for about 1 hour, or until just frozen.

Meanwhile, cook the rice according to packet instructions. Make a flat omelette with the eggs, salt and pepper and 1½ teaspoons oil (see page 18). Slide the omelette out of the pan on to a plate or board and roll up tightly; set aside. Pound the chilli in a pestle and mortar with the onion and garlic or with the end of a straight wooden rolling pin.

Drain the rice. Cut the pork on the diagonal into 5 mm (¼ inch) thick slices, then cut the slices into thin strips. Heat the wok until hot. Add the remaining oil and heat over a moderate heat until hot. Add the pounded mixture and stir-fry over a gentle heat for 2-3 minutes to blend the flavours without browning the ingredients. Add the meat, increase the heat to high and stir-fry for 3 minutes. Add the prawns and stir-fry for a further 1 minute, or until the pork is tender. Add the rice and the remaining ingredients and stir-fry for about 2 minutes until evenly mixed.

Transfer the nasi goreng to a serving dish. Slice the rolled omelette into thin rings, then arrange on top. Garnish with parsley and serve.

SERVES 4

Nutritional content per serving: Carbohydrate: 90   Fat: 23   Fibre: 3   Kilocalories: 775

Lamb and courgette fritters

2 large courgettes, cut into 12 rounds
3-4 tablespoons plain flour seasoned with salt and pepper
2 tablespoons sesame seeds
50 g (2 oz) minced lamb
1 spring onion, chopped finely
1 clove garlic, crushed
vegetable oil for deep frying
2 eggs (size 1 or 2), beaten
parsley sprigs to garnish

Coat the courgette rounds in the seasoned flour.

Put the sesame seeds in the wok and dry-fry over a moderate heat for 1-2 minutes until toasted then remove and set aside.

Mix the minced lamb with the spring onion, garlic and toasted sesame seeds. Press on to one side of each courgette round, then coat in more seasoned flour.

Pour enough oil into the wok for deep frying and heat to 190°C, 375°F or until a cube of bread browns in 30 seconds. Dip the courgette rings into the beaten eggs a few at a time, then deep fry in batches until golden brown, turning them over once. Lift out of the oil with a slotted spoon, drain on kitchen paper and keep hot while deep frying the remainder. Garnish with parsley and serve warm.

MAKES 24

Nutritional content per fritter: Carbohydrate: 2   Fat: 4   Kilocalories: 45

Lamb and Courgette Fritters; Nasi Goreng

STIR-FRIED PORK WITH CUCUMBER

375 g (12 oz) pork fillet (tenderloin)
1 cucumber
1 tablespoon cornflour
150 ml (¼ pint) cold chicken stock or water
2 tablespoons soy sauce
2 tablespoons dry sherry or sherry vinegar
1 tablespoon vegetable oil
1 onion, sliced thinly
2.5 cm (1 inch) piece fresh root ginger, peeled
   and cut into matchsticks
salt and pepper

Wrap the pork and place in the freezer for about 1 hour, or until just frozen. Cut on the diagonal into 5 mm (¼ inch) thick slices, then cut the slices into thin strips. Trim off the ends of the cucumber, then cut into 6 equal pieces. Cut each of these pieces into quarters lengthways; cut off and discard the seeds.

Blend the cornflour in a jug with 2 tablespoons of the stock or water, then add the remaining stock or water, the soy sauce and sherry or vinegar. Stir well to combine.

Heat the wok until hot. Add the oil and heat over a moderate heat until hot. Add the onion and ginger and stir-fry for a few seconds, then add the meat, increase the heat to high and stir-fry for 2-3 minutes.

Pour in the cornflour mixture and bring to the boil over a high heat, stirring constantly until thickened and glossy. Add the cucumber and stir-fry for 1-2 minutes or until the meat is tender and the cucumber is hot. Add salt and pepper to taste and serve at once.

SERVES 4

Nutritional content per serving: Carbohydrate: 8   Fat: 10   Fibre: 1   Kilocalories: 245

PORK WITH PEAS

375 g (12 oz) pork fillet (tenderloin)
1 tablespoon olive or vegetable oil
1 Spanish onion, quartered and sliced thinly
1 tablespoon tomato purée
2 teaspoons paprika
½ teaspoon chilli powder
¼ teaspoon caster sugar
125 ml (4 fl oz) dry white wine
250 g (8 oz) frozen petits pois
2 cloves garlic, crushed
2 tablespoons chopped fresh coriander or
   parsley
salt and pepper

Wrap the pork and place in the freezer for about 1 hour, or until just frozen, then cut on the diagonal into 5 mm (¼ inch) thick slices.

Heat the wok until hot. Add the oil and heat over a moderate heat until hot. Add the pork and onion slices, increase the heat to high and stir-fry for 2-3 minutes. Remove with a slotted spoon and set aside on a plate.

Remove the wok from the heat and add the tomato purée, paprika, chilli powder and sugar. Stir well to combine, then gradually stir in the wine. Return the wok to the heat, bring to the boil, stirring, then add the frozen peas, garlic and salt and pepper to taste. Lower the heat and simmer for 5 minutes or until the peas are cooked and the sauce has reduced, stirring frequently.

Return the meat and onion mixture to the wok, together with any juices, and increase the heat to high. Stir-fry for 1-2 minutes until the meat is tender and coated in the sauce mixture. Remove from the heat, stir in the coriander or parsley and serve at once.

SERVES 4

Nutritional content per serving: Carbohydrate: 7   Fat: 25   Fibre: 8   Kilocalories: 350

Pork with Peas; Stir-Fried Pork with Cucumber (top); Ants Climbing Trees

ANTS CLIMBING TREES

THIS DISH GETS ITS NAME FROM THE MINCED PORK (ANTS) CLINGING TO THE NOODLES (TREES). TRANSPARENT OR CELLOPHANE NOODLES ARE THE TRADITIONAL NOODLES USED, BUT ORDINARY EGG NOODLES ARE JUST AS GOOD

250 g (8 oz) minced pork
1 × 198 g (7 oz) packet fine egg noodles
2 tablespoons groundnut or vegetable oil
4 spring onions, trimmed and chopped finely
250 ml (8 fl oz) hot chicken stock
2 spring onions, finely chopped, to garnish
MARINADE:
2 tablespoons soy sauce
1 tablespoon dry sherry or sherry vinegar
1 tablespoon groundnut or vegetable oil
1 teaspoon sesame oil
1 teaspoon chilli sauce
½ teaspoon sugar
pinch of salt

Whisk the marinade ingredients together in a bowl. Add the pork and stir well to mix. Cover and leave to marinate for about 30 minutes.

Meanwhile, cook the noodles according to packet instructions; drain thoroughly.

Heat the wok until hot. Add the oil and heat over a moderate heat until hot. Add the pork and spring onions and stir-fry for about 5 minutes or until the meat loses its pink colour. Pour in the stock and bring to the boil, stirring constantly, then add the drained noodles. Stir-fry for 1 minute or until all of the liquid is absorbed and the noodles are hot. Sprinkle with the spring onions and serve at once.

SERVES 3-4

Nutritional content per serving: Carbohydrate: 50   Fat: 41   Fibre: 4   Kilocalories: 660

PAPER-THIN LAMB WITH GARLIC AND SPRING ONIONS

500 g (1 lb) lamb neck fillet
2 tablespoons groundnut or vegetable oil
3 large cloves garlic, sliced thinly
½ teaspoon chilli powder, or to taste
½ teaspoon soft dark brown sugar
pinch of salt
1 large bunch spring onions, cut into 7.5 cm
  (3 inch) lengths, then shredded lengthways
2 tablespoons soy sauce
2 tablespoons dry sherry or sherry vinegar
2 teaspoons sesame oil

Wrap the lamb and place in the freezer for about 1 hour, or until just frozen, then cut into thin strips across the grain, discarding any fat.

Heat the wok until hot. Add the groundnut or vegetable oil and heat over a moderate heat until hot. Add the garlic and stir-fry over a gentle heat for a few seconds to flavour the oil, then add the meat and sprinkle over the chilli powder, sugar and salt. Increase the heat to high and stir-fry for 3-4 minutes until the meat is browned on all sides. Add the spring onions, the soy sauce and sherry or vinegar and stir-fry for 1-2 minutes or until the meat is tender and all the ingredients are quite dry. Serve at once, sprinkled with the sesame oil.

SERVES 4

Nutritional content per serving: Carbohydrate: 4   Fat: 19   Kilocalories: 315

QUICK-FRIED LAMB WITH LEEKS

1 × 375 g (12 oz) slices leg of lamb
3 tablespoons groundnut or vegetable oil
4 leeks, cut diagonally into 4 cm (1½ inch)
  lengths, washed, drained and dried
2.5 cm (1 inch) piece fresh root ginger,
  peeled and chopped finely
2 cloves garlic, crushed
2 tablespoons soy sauce
2 teaspoons wine vinegar
1 teaspoon Chinese five-spice powder
½ teaspoon soft dark brown sugar
¼ teaspoon salt
parsley sprigs to garnish

Wrap the lamb and place in the freezer for about 1 hour, or until just frozen, then cut into thin strips across the grain, discarding any fat and sinew.

Heat the wok until hot. Add the oil and heat over a moderate heat until hot. Add the meat, increase the heat to high and stir-fry for 2-3 minutes until browned on all sides. Add the leeks, ginger and garlic and stir-fry for 1 minute, then add the soy sauce, vinegar, half of the five-spice powder, the sugar and salt. Stir-fry for 30 seconds to 1 minute until the meat is tender and all the ingredients are evenly combined. Garnish with parsley and serve at once, sprinkled with the remaining five-spice powder.

SERVES 4

Nutritional content per serving: Carbohydrate: 7   Fat: 19   Fibre: 2   Kilocalories: 280

Quick-Fried Lamb with Leeks; Paper-Thin Lamb with Garlic and Spring Onions (top); Vietnamese Pork Parcels

VIETNAMESE PORK PARCELS

THESE ARE THE VIETNAMESE EQUIVALENT OF CHINESE SPRING ROLLS. INSTEAD OF USING WRAPPERS MADE FROM DOUGH THAT ARE DEEP-FRIED, THESE PORK PARCELS USE LETTUCE LEAVES TO ENCLOSE THEIR FILLING. THE RESULT IS FRESHER AND HEALTHIER

2 tablespoons groundnut or vegetable oil
350 g (12 oz) minced pork
5 cm (2 inch) piece fresh root ginger, peeled and chopped finely
2 cloves garlic, chopped finely
4 spring onions, chopped finely
200 ml (7 fl oz) fish or chicken stock
2 tablespoons soy sauce
2 teaspoons soft dark brown sugar
125 g (4 oz) cooked peeled prawns, defrosted and dried thoroughly, if frozen, chopped roughly
1 teaspoon anchovy extract
½ teaspoon chilli powder, or to taste
salt and pepper
1 bunch fresh mint and/or basil leaves
16 crisp lettuce leaves, such as lollo rosso

Heat the wok until hot. Add the oil and heat over a moderate heat until hot. Add the pork, ginger, garlic and spring onions and stir-fry for about 5 minutes or until the meat loses its pink colour.

Add the stock, soy sauce and sugar and stir-fry until the stock is absorbed. Add the prawns, anchovy extract and chilli powder and stir-fry for 1-2 minutes until the prawns are heated through. Add salt and pepper to taste and serve at once. Guests then place a few mint or basil leaves inside each lettuce leaf and top with the pork mixture. The lettuce is then rolled up around the filling and the parcel is eaten with the fingers.

SERVES 4

Nutritional content per serving: Carbohydrate: 7   Fat: 28   Fibre: 2   Kilocalories: 530

HOT AND SOUR PORK

PROTEIN-PACKED TOFU (BEAN CURD) MAKES A LITTLE MEAT GO A LONG WAY IN THIS COLOURFUL DISH. VEGETABLES ARE INCLUDED TOO, SO THE ONLY ACCOMPANIMENT NEEDED IS BOILED RICE TO PROVIDE A COMPLETE MEAL.

375 g (12 oz) pork fillet (tenderloin)
3 tablespoons soy sauce
2 tablespoons cider vinegar
2 teaspoons cornflour
2.5 cm (1 inch) piece fresh root ginger, peeled
1 large clove garlic
2 dried red chillies, chopped roughly
1 × 297 g (10.5 oz) packet tofu (bean curd), drained and dried
4 tablespoons groundnut or vegetable oil
1 large red pepper, cored, deseeded and cut lengthways into thin strips
250 g (8 oz) mangetout
125 ml (4 fl oz) chicken stock
1-2 tablespoons chilli sauce, according to taste
salt and pepper
coriander sprigs to garnish

Wrap the pork and place in the freezer for about 1 hour, or until just frozen, then cut on the diagonal into 5 mm (1/4 inch) thick slices. Place the slices in a bowl, add the soy sauce, vinegar and cornflour and stir well to mix. Set aside.

Pound the ginger and garlic in a pestle and mortar or process in a food processor or blender with the chillies. Cut the tofu into slices roughly the same size as the pork.

Heat the wok until hot. Add 1 tablespoon oil and heat over a moderate heat until hot. Add the red pepper and mangetout, sprinkle with salt and pepper to taste and stir-fry for 3 minutes. Remove with a slotted spoon and set aside.

Heat 2 tablespoons oil in the wok, add the tofu and stir-fry carefully over a moderate heat for 1-2 minutes until lightly coloured on both sides. Remove with a slotted spoon, drain on kitchen paper and keep hot.

Heat the remaining oil in the wok, add the pounded mixture and stir-fry over a gentle heat for 2-3 minutes to blend the flavours without browning the ingredients. Add about half of the meat, increase the heat to high and stir-fry for 2-3 minutes. Remove with a slotted spoon and set aside on a plate. Repeat with the remaining meat.

Pour the stock into the wok and bring to the boil over a high heat, stirring constantly, then stir in the chilli sauce. Return the meat and any juices to the wok with the red pepper and mangetout. Stir-fry for 1-2 minutes until the meat is tender and all the ingredients are hot and evenly combined. Gently fold in the tofu, garnish with coriander and serve at once.

SERVES 4

Nutritional content per serving: Carbohydrate: 7   Fat: 24   Fibre: 2   Kilocalories: 390

Hot and Sour Pork; Sweet and Sour Minced Pork

Sweet and sour minced pork

SERVED IN CHICORY LEAVES, THIS SPICY MINCED PORK MAKES AN ATTRACTIVE STARTER FOR A DINNER PARTY WITH AN ORIENTAL THEME

3 dried red chillies

1 tablespoon groundnut or vegetable oil

250 g (8 oz) minced pork

1 tablespoon soy sauce

1 tablespoon soft dark brown sugar

2 teaspoons dry sherry or sherry vinegar

½ × 510 g (1 lb 2 oz) jar bean sprout salad in wine vinegar

½ × 200 g (7 oz) packet creamed coconut

2 tablespoons chopped fresh coriander

16 large chicory leaves (about 1 large head chicory)

2 teaspoons sesame oil

salt

parsley to garnish

Put the dried red chillies in the wok and dry-fry over a moderate heat for 2-3 minutes. Transfer to a mortar and crush with a pestle or use the end of a straight wooden rolling pin.

Heat the oil in the wok until hot. Add the pork and pounded chillies and stir-fry over a moderate heat for about 5 minutes or until the meat loses its pink colour. Add the soy sauce, sugar and sherry or vinegar and stir-fry for 1 minute until blended with the meat.

Stir in the bean sprout salad with its liquid and bring to the boil. Crumble in the creamed coconut, stir-fry until blended, then lower the heat and simmer for 10-15 minutes until thickened, stirring frequently. Remove from the heat and stir in the chopped coriander and salt to taste.

Arrange the chicory leaves in a circle on a large round serving platter. Spoon in the pork mixture, sprinkle with the sesame oil and garnish with the parsley. Serve at once.

SERVES 4

Nutritional content per serving: Carbohydrate: 12   Fat: 28   Fibre: 1   Kilocalories: 385

RAINBOW PORK

375 g (12 oz) pork fillet (tenderloin)
1 × 250 g (8.82 oz) packet fine egg noodles
250 g (8 oz) fresh spinach or Chinese leaves
2 teaspoons cornflour
8 tablespoons cold chicken stock or water
4 tablespoons soy sauce
2 tablespoons dry sherry or sherry vinegar
1 teaspoon soft light or dark brown sugar
2 tablespoons groundnut or vegetable oil
1 tablespoon butter or margarine
1 × 454 g (1 lb) packet frozen stir-fry
   vegetable mix with mangetout
2 cloves garlic, crushed
salt and pepper

Wrap the pork and place in the freezer for about 1 hour, or until just frozen. Meanwhile, cook the noodles according to packet instructions. Drain. Remove the stalks and any tough ribs from the spinach. Put several spinach leaves one on top of another, roll them up together into a cigar shape, then cut crossways into shreds. (If using Chinese leaves, simply shred them in the usual way.)

Blend the cornflour in a jug with 2 tablespoons of the stock or water, then add the remaining stock or water, the soy sauce, sherry or vinegar and sugar. Stir well to combine. Cut the pork on the diagonal into 5 mm (1/4 inch) thick slices, then cut the slices into thin strips. Heat the wok until hot. Add the oil and heat over a moderate heat until hot. Add the meat, increase the heat to high and stir-fry for 2-3 minutes. Remove with a slotted spoon and set aside on a plate.

Add the butter or margarine to the wok and heat until melted, then add the frozen vegetables and garlic and stir-fry according to packet instructions. Add the spinach or Chinese leaves and stir-fry for 30 seconds, then pour in the cornflour mixture and bring to the boil over a high heat, stirring constantly until thickened and glossy. Return the meat and juices to the wok with the noodles and stir-fry for 1-2 minutes until the meat is tender and all the ingredients are hot and evenly combined. Add salt and pepper to taste and serve at once.

SERVES 4

Nutritional content per serving: Carbohydrate: 63   Fat: 24   Fibre: 8   Kilocalories: 620

HONEY GLAZED PORK

500 g (1 lb) pork fillet (tenderloin)
2 tablespoons groundnut or vegetable oil
2 tablespoons flaked almonds
1 clove garlic, crushed
parsley sprigs to garnish
GLAZE:
2 teaspoons cornflour
2 tablespoons water
2 tablespoons clear honey
1 tablesoon soy sauce
1 tablespoon dry sherry or sherry vinegar
1/2 teaspoon ground ginger
1/4 teaspoon ground cinnamon
1 large pinch ground cloves

Wrap the pork and place in the freezer for about 1 hour, or until just frozen. Cut on the diagonal into 5 mm (1/4 inch) thick slices, then cut the slices into thin strips.

Prepare the glaze: blend the cornflour in a jug with the water, then add the remaining glaze ingredients. Stir well to combine.

Heat the wok until hot. Add the oil and heat over a moderate heat until hot. Add the almonds and stir-fry for 2-3 minutes until golden brown, then remove with a slotted spoon and drain on kitchen paper.

Add the meat and garlic to the oil, increase the heat to high and stir-fry for 2-3 minutes. Pour in the glaze mixture and bring to the boil, stirring constantly until thickened and glossy. Stir-fry for 1-2 minutes or until the meat is tender and coated with the glaze. Garnish with parsley and serve at once, sprinkled with the almonds.

SERVES 4

Nutritional content per serving: Carbohydrate: 6   Fat: 20   Fibre: 2   Kilocalories: 370

Rainbow Pork; Honey Glazed Pork (top); Deep-Fried Crispy Lamb

DEEP-FRIED CRISPY LAMB

500 g (1 lb) lamb neck fillet
1 egg white
2 cloves garlic, crushed
1 tablespoon cornflour
½ teaspoon Chinese five-spice powder
vegetable oil for deep frying
3 spring onions, sliced thinly
SAUCE:
2 teaspoons cornflour
4 tablespoons water
2 tablespoons soft dark brown sugar
2 tablespoons soy sauce
1 tablespoon dry sherry
1 tablespoon wine vinegar
2 teaspoons chilli sauce, or to taste

Wrap the lamb and place in the freezer for about 1 hour, or until just frozen, then cut into 1 cm (½ inch) cubes. Lightly beat the egg white in a shallow dish with half of the crushed garlic, the cornflour and five-spice powder. Add the cubes of lamb and turn to coat. Cover and leave to stand for 30 minutes.

Meanwhile, prepare the sauce: blend the cornflour in a jug with 1 tablespoon of the water, then add the remaining water, the sugar, soy sauce, sherry, vinegar and chilli sauce. Stir well to combine.

Pour enough oil into the wok for deep frying and heat to 190°C, 375°F or until a cube of bread browns in 30 seconds. Add a few cubes of lamb and deep fry for about 4 minutes or until golden brown and crisp. Lift out of the oil with a slotted spoon and drain on kitchen paper while deep frying the remainder

Carefully pour all but 1-2 tablespoons of oil out of the wok. Add the remaining garlic and stir-fry over a gentle heat for a few seconds to flavour the oil. Pour in the sauce mixture and bring to the boil over a high heat, stirring constantly until thickened and glossy. Add the meat and toss over a high heat for 30 seconds or until coated in the sauce. Serve at once, sprinkled with the spring onions.

SERVES 4

Nutritional content per serving: Carbohydrate: 2   Fat: 17   Kilocalories: 295

LAMB WITH WALNUTS AND YELLOW BEAN SAUCE

500 g (1 lb) lamb neck fillet
2 tablespoons groundnut or vegetable oil
1 large Spanish onion, quartered and sliced
  thinly
2 large cloves garlic, crushed
4 tablespoons yellow bean sauce
50 g (2 oz) walnut pieces
salt and pepper

Wrap the lamb and place in the freezer for about 1 hour, or until just frozen, then cut into thin strips across the grain, discarding any fat.

Heat the wok until hot. Add the oil and heat over a moderate heat until hot. Add the onion and stir-fry for 2-3 minutes until softened. Add the meat and garlic, increase the heat to high and stir-fry for 3-4 minutes until the meat is browned. Add the yellow bean sauce and salt and pepper to taste, then toss the meat for 1-2 minutes until tender and coated in the sauce. Add the walnuts, stir-fry for 30 seconds and serve.

SERVES 4

Nutritional content per serving: Carbohydrate: 6   Fat: 23   Fibre: 2   Kilocalories: 375

CRISPY PORK WITH ORANGE AND VEGETABLES

500 g (1 lb) pork fillet (tenderloin)
125 g (4 oz) whole baby sweetcorn cobs
125 g (4 oz) baby carrots
125 g (4 oz) green beans, halved if large
1 egg white
1 tablespoon cornflour
vegetable oil for shallow frying
4 spring onions, sliced thinly on the diagonal
2.5 cm (1 inch) piece fresh root ginger,
  chopped finely
1-2 cloves garlic, crushed
salt and pepper
SAUCE:
2 teaspoons cornflour
6 tablespoons cold chicken stock or water
finely grated rind and juice of 1 large orange
2 tablespoons soy sauce
¼ teaspoon Chinese five-spice powder

Wrap the pork and place in the freezer for about 1 hour, or until just frozen. Cut the pork on the diagonal into 5 mm (¼ inch) thick slices, then cut the slices into thin strips.

Bring a large pan of water to the boil, add a pinch of salt and the baby sweetcorn. Bring back to the boil and simmer for 3 minutes. Remove the sweetcorn. Repeat with the carrots, then the green beans, allowing only 2 minutes' cooking for the beans.

Prepare the sauce: blend the cornflour with 2 tablespoons of the stock or water, then add the remaining stock or water, orange rind and juice, soy sauce and five-spice powder. Stir well.

Lightly beat the egg white with the cornflour and a pinch of salt. Add the pork and turn to coat. Pour enough oil into the wok to come 2.5-4 cm (1-1½ inches) up the sides. Heat over a moderate heat until hot but not smoking. Shallow fry the pork a few strips at a time for about 2-3 minutes or until crispy. Lift out with a slotted spoon, drain on kitchen paper and keep hot while frying the remainder.

Carefully pour all but 1-2 tablespoons of oil out of the wok. Add the spring onions, ginger and garlic and stir-fry over a gentle heat for 2-3 minutes to blend the flavours without browning the ingredients. Add the parboiled vegetables, increase the heat to high and stir-fry until heated through. Pour in the cornflour mixture and bring to the boil over a high heat, stirring constantly until thickened and glossy. Add salt and pepper to taste. Serve at once, topped with the crispy pork.

SERVES 4

Nutritional content per serving: Carbohydrate: 5   Fat: 23   Fibre: 2   Kilocalories: 375

Lamb with Walnuts and Yellow Bean Sauce; Crispy Pork with Orange and Vegetables; Oriental Pork with Tofu

ORIENTAL PORK WITH TOFU

TAKE CARE WHEN STIR-FRYING TOFU (BEAN CURD) AS IT HAS A TENDENCY TO BREAK UP, ESPECIALLY AROUND THE EDGES

250 g (8 oz) pork fillet (tenderloin)
2 tablespoons groundnut or vegetable oil
2 cloves garlic, crushed
1 × 297 g (10.5 oz) packet tofu (bean
  curd), drained, dried and cut into cubes
250 g (8 oz) mooli, peeled and cut into
  matchsticks
125 g (4 oz) mangetout
250 g (8 oz) Chinese leaves, shredded
1 teaspoon sesame oil
SAUCE:
2 teaspoons cornflour
6 tablespoons cold chicken stock or water
2 tablespoons soy sauce
2 tablespoons dry sherry or sherry vinegar
2 teaspoons lemon juice
½ teaspoon Chinese five-spice powder
½ teaspoon chilli powder, or to taste
pinch of salt

Wrap the pork and place in the freezer for about 1 hour, or until just frozen. Cut on the diagonal into 5 mm (¼ inch) thick slices, then cut the slices into thin strips.

Prepare the sauce: blend the cornflour in a jug with 2 tablespoons of the stock or water, then add the remaining stock or water and the remaining sauce ingredients. Stir well to combine.

Heat the wok until hot. Add the groundnut or vegetable oil and heat over a moderate heat until hot. Add the pork and garlic, increase the heat to high and stir-fry for 2-3 minutes. Remove with a slotted spoon and set aside on a plate.

Add the tofu to the wok and stir-fry carefully over a moderate heat for 1-2 minutes until lightly coloured on all sides. Remove with a slotted spoon, drain on kitchen paper and keep hot.

Add the mooli and mangetout to the wok and stir-fry for 2 minutes, then add the Chinese leaves and stir-fry for 1 minute longer. Pour in the sauce mixture and bring to the boil over a high heat, stirring constantly until thickened and glossy. Return the meat and any juices to the wok and stir-fry for 1-2 minutes until the meat is tender and evenly combined with the vegetables. Gently fold in the tofu and serve at once, sprinkled with the sesame oil.

SERVES 4

Nutritional content per serving: Carbohydrate: 8   Fat: 16   Fibre: 3   Kilocalories: 280

LAMB'S LIVER WITH LEEKS AND SPRING ONIONS

1 teaspoon cornflour

1 tablespoon soy sauce

½ teaspoon Chinese five-spice powder

¼-½ teaspoon chilli powder, according to taste

250 g (8 oz) lamb's liver, cut into 4 cm × 5 mm (1½ × ¼ inch) strips

2 tablespoons groundnut or vegetable oil

1 clove garlic, crushed

2 leeks, shredded

4 spring onions, shredded

salt and pepper

SAUCE:

2 teaspoons cornflour

2 tablespoons water

2 tablespoons dry sherry or sherry vinegar

2 teaspoons soy sauce

1 teaspoon caster sugar

1 teaspoon sesame oil

Whisk the cornflour in a bowl with the soy sauce, five-spice powder and chilli powder. Add the strips of liver and turn to coat. Cover and leave to marinate for 30 minutes.

Prepare the sauce: blend the cornflour in a jug with the water, then add the sherry or vinegar, soy sauce, sugar and sesame oil. Stir well to combine.

Heat the wok until hot. Add the oil and heat over a moderate heat until hot. Add the liver and garlic and stir-fry for 2-3 minutes until the liver is browned on all sides. Remove with a slotted spoon and set aside on a plate.

Heat the remaining oil in the wok. Add the leeks and spring onions and stir-fry over a gentle heat for 1 minute. Pour in the sauce mixture and bring to the boil over a high heat, stirring constantly until thickened and glossy. Return the liver and any juices to the wok and add salt and pepper to taste. Stir-fry for 30 seconds or until the liver is evenly coated in the sauce. Serve at once.

SERVES 2

Nutritional content per serving: Carbohydrate: 8   Fat: 16   Fibre: 1   Kilocalories: 235

SZECHUAN PORK

SZECHUAN DISHES ARE HOT AND SPICY, SO INCLUDE AS MANY OF THE FRESH CHILLI SEEDS IN THIS DISH AS YOU DARE!

500 g (1 lb) pork fillet (tenderloin)

3 tablespoons groundnut or vegetable oil

1 green pepper, cored, deseeded and cut lengthways into thin strips

2.5 cm (1 inch) piece fresh root ginger, peeled and chopped finely

2 cloves garlic, chopped finely

2 fresh green chillies, chopped roughly, seeds discarded according to taste

1 × 227 g (8 oz) can sliced bamboo shoots, drained

SAUCE:

2 teaspoons cornflour

6 tablespoons cold chicken stock or water

2 tablespoons chilli sauce

2 tablespoons dry sherry or sherry vinegar

1 tablespoon soy sauce

2 teaspoons soft dark brown sugar

pinch of salt

Wrap the pork and place in the freezer for about 1 hour, or until just frozen. Cut on the diagonal into 5 mm (¼ inch) thick slices, then cut the slices into thin strips.

Prepare the sauce: blend the cornflour in a jug with 2 tablespoons of the stock or water, then add the remaining stock or water and the remaining sauce ingredients. Stir well to combine.

Heat the wok until hot. Add the oil and heat over a moderate heat until hot. Add the pork, increase the heat to high and stir-fry for 2-3 minutes, then remove with a slotted spoon and set aside on a plate.

Add the green pepper, ginger, garlic and chillies and stir-fry for 1 minute, then pour in the sauce mixture and bring to the boil over a high heat, stirring constantly until thickened and glossy.

Return the meat and any juices to the wok with the bamboo shoots and stir-fry over a high heat for 1-2 minutes until the meat is tender and the bamboo shoots are hot. Serve at once.

SERVES 4

Nutritional content per serving: Carbohydrate: 10   Fat: 20   Fibre: 2   Kilocalories: 370

Lamb's Liver with Leeks and Spring Onions; Szechuan Pork; Yellow Flower Lamb

YELLOW FLOWER LAMB

THE PRETTY OMELETTE GARNISH ON TOP OF THIS SIMPLE STIR-FRIED DISH GIVES IT ITS NAME

375 g (12 oz) lamb neck fillet
2 eggs
4 spring onions, chopped finely
2½ tablespoons groundnut or vegetable oil
10 g (½ oz) dried sliced mushrooms
2.5 cm (1 inch) piece fresh root ginger, peeled
  and chopped finely
½ × 175 g (6 oz) can sliced bamboo shoots,
  drained
2 tablespoons soy sauce
2 tablespoons dry sherry or sherry vinegar
1 teaspoon soft dark brown sugar
½ teaspoon Chinese five-spice powder
1 tablespoon sesame oil
salt and pepper

Wrap the lamb and place in the freezer for about 1 hour, or until just frozen.

Beat the eggs in a bowl with half of the spring onions and salt and pepper to taste. Make a flat omelette with the eggs, salt and pepper and 1½ teaspoons oil (see page 18). Slide the omelette out of the pan on to a plate or board and roll up tightly; set aside.

Cook the dried mushrooms in boiling water for 10 minutes, or according to the packet instructions. Drain. Cut the lamb into thin strips across the grain, discarding any fat and sinew.

Heat the wok until hot. Add the remaining oil and heat over a moderate heat until hot. Add the remaining spring onions and the ginger and stir-fry over a gentle heat for a few seconds to flavour the oil. Add the meat, increase the heat to high and stir-fry for 2-3 minutes until browned on all sides. Add the mushrooms, bamboo shoots, soy sauce, sherry or vinegar, sugar and five-spice powder. Stir-fry for 1-2 minutes or until the meat is tender and all the ingredients are hot and evenly combined.

Transfer the lamb to a warmed serving dish. Slice the rolled omelette into thin rings, then arrange on top to resemble flower petals. Sprinkle over the sesame oil and serve at once.

SERVES 4

Nutritional content per serving: Carbohydrate: 10   Fat: 24   Fibre: 1   Kilocalories: 365

Vegetables

STIR-FRIED VEGETABLES ARE SO CRISP, CRUNCHY AND COLOURFUL THAT NO ORIENTAL MEAL SEEMS COMPLETE WITHOUT THEM. IN THIS CHAPTER YOU WILL FIND SUCH A VARIETY OF VEGETABLE ACCOMPANIMENTS AND MAIN COURSES THAT YOU WILL HARDLY KNOW WHICH TO CHOOSE FIRST.

FRAGRANT RICE

RICE COOKED IN COCONUT MILK RATHER THAN WATER HAS A RICH FLAVOUR AND CREAMY TEXTURE. THE COCONUT MILK DOES TEND TO MAKE THE RICE STICK TO THE BOTTOM OF THE WOK, HOWEVER. TO PREVENT THIS, USE A HEAT DIFFUSING MAT UNDERNEATH THE WOK. IF COOKING ON ELECTRICITY, PLACE THE WOK ON A COLD RING AFTER REMOVING THE FLAVOURINGS AND SET VERY LOW

1 × 200 g (7 oz) packet creamed coconut
600 ml (1 pint) boiling water
3 tablespoons desiccated coconut
250 g (8 oz) long-grain rice
thinly pared rind of 1 large lemon
1 bay leaf
1 cinnamon stick
6 cloves
few strands saffron
¼ teaspoon salt
deep-fried onion rings to garnish (optional)

Dissolve the creamed coconut in the boiling water to make coconut milk; set aside.

Place the desiccated coconut in the wok and dry-fry for a few minutes until golden brown. Transfer to a bowl and set aside.

Rinse the rice in a sieve under cold running water. Pour the coconut milk into the wok, add the rice, lemon rind, bay leaf, cinnamon stick, cloves, saffron and salt. Bring to the boil over moderate heat, stirring constantly.

Lower the heat, cover and simmer gently for 10 minutes. Discard the flavourings which have risen to the surface of the rice. Stir the rice, then cover tightly and simmer very gently for 20 minutes, without stirring or even lifting the lid. Before serving, fluff the rice up with a fork. Garnish with the toasted coconut, and deep-fried onion rings if you like.

SERVES 4

Nutritional content per serving: Carbohydrate: 58   Fat: 25   Fibre: 5   Kilocalories: 460

SWEET SPINACH WITH GARLIC AND SESAME SEEDS

250 g (8 oz) fresh spinach leaves
3-4 cloves garlic, crushed
2 tablespoons soy sauce
2 teaspoons clear honey
2 tablespoons sesame seeds
2 tablespoons sesame oil
salt and pepper

Remove the stalks and any tough ribs from the spinach. Put several spinach leaves one on top of another, roll them up together into a cigar shape, then using a sharp knife, cut crossways into shreds. Repeat with the remaining leaves.

Whisk the garlic in a jug with the soy sauce and honey.

Put the sesame seeds in the wok and dry-fry over a moderate heat for 1-2 minutes until lightly toasted. Remove from the wok and set aside.

Heat the oil in the wok until hot but not smoking, add the spinach and increase the heat to high. Stir-fry for 1-2 minutes until the spinach just begins to wilt, then add the soy sauce mixture and season to taste. Stir-fry for a further 30 seconds. Serve at once, sprinkled with the toasted sesame seeds.

SERVES 4

Nutritional content per serving: Carbohydrate: 10   Fat: 16   Fibre: 5   Kilocalories: 195

Fragrant Rice (top); Sweet Spinach with Garlic and Sesame Seeds

TEMPURA

sunflower oil for deep frying
8 button mushrooms
1 red pepper, cored, deseeded and sliced
   lengthways into 16 strips
1 green pepper, cored, deseeded and sliced
   lengthways into 16 strips
4 courgettes, sliced into rounds
BATTER:
150 g (5 oz) plain flour
2 tablespoons arrowroot or cornflour
pinch of salt
300 ml (½ pint) iced water
DIPPING SAUCE:
4 tablespoons soy sauce
4 tablespoons dry sherry
1 tablespoon finely chopped fresh root
   ginger
pinch mustard powder
½ teaspoon caster sugar

First make the batter: sift the plain flour, arrowroot or cornflour into a bowl with the salt. Add the water a little at a time, whisking constantly. Cover and place in the refrigerator to chill for 30 minutes.

Whisk the dipping sauce ingredients together in a bowl. Pour enough oil into the wok for deep-frying and heat to 190°C, 375°F or until a cube of bread browns in 30 seconds. Using a slotted spoon, dip a few pieces of each vegetable into the batter, then lift them out, making sure there is plenty of batter around them.

Lower the vegetables gently into the hot oil and deep fry for 2-3 minutes until crisp. Lift out with a slotted spoon, drain on kitchen paper and keep hot while deep frying the remainder. Whisk the dipping sauce again, then divide equally between 4 individual dipping bowls. Serve the tempura at once, with the bowls of dipping sauce on the side.

SERVES 4

Nutritional content per serving: Carbohydrate: 40   Fat: 18   Fibre: 4   Kilocalories: 360

CARROTS AND GINGER WITH BEAN SPROUTS

2 tablespoons olive or walnut oil
1 medium onion, sliced thinly
2.5 cm (1 inch) piece fresh root ginger, peeled
   and cut into matchsticks
375 g (12 oz) young carrots, cut into
   matchsticks
250 g (8 oz) bean sprouts
finely grated rind and juice of 1 orange
1 teaspoon caster sugar
salt and pepper
parsley sprigs to garnish

Heat the wok until hot. Add the oil and heat over a moderate heat until hot but not smoking. Add the onion and ginger and stir-fry for 2-3 minutes until the onion softens slightly, then add the carrots and stir-fry for 3 minutes. Add the bean sprouts, orange rind and juice and sugar. Season to taste. Increase the heat to high and stir-fry until the bean sprouts are hot and evenly combined with the carrots. Garnish with parsley and serve at once.

SERVES 4

Nutritional content per serving: Carbohydrate: 9   Fat: 9   Fibre: 4   Kilocalories: 100

Carrots and Ginger with Bean Sprouts; Tempura (top); Green Beans with Broccoli and Almonds

GREEN BEANS WITH BROCCOLI AND ALMONDS

2 teaspoons cornflour
6 tablespoons cold vegetable stock or water
2 tablespoons soy sauce
1 tablespoon lemon juice
4 tablespoons flaked almonds
2 tablespoons groundnut or vegetable oil
175 g (6 oz) broccoli, florets separated, stalks sliced thinly on the diagonal
175 g (6 oz) green beans, cut diagonally into 4.5 cm (1½-2 inch) lengths
3 cloves garlic, crushed
pepper

Blend the cornflour in a jug with 2 tablespoons of the stock or water, then add the remaining stock or water and the soy sauce and lemon juice. Stir well to combine.

Put the flaked almonds in the wok and dry-fry over a moderate heat for 1-2 minutes until toasted. Remove from the wok and set aside on a plate.

Heat the oil in the wok, add the broccoli and stir-fry for 3 minutes. Add the beans and garlic and stir-fry for 3-4 minutes. Pour in the cornflour mixture and bring to the boil over a high heat, stirring constantly until thickened and glossy. Add pepper to taste and serve at once, sprinkled with the toasted almonds.

SERVES 4

Nutritional content per serving: Carbohydrate: 8   Fat: 15   Fibre: 5   Kilocalories: 185

TAHU GORENG

THIS HOT AND SPICY INDONESIAN DISH MAKES A FILLING AND NUTRITIOUS LUNCH OR SUPPER WHEN SERVED WITH NOODLES OR RICE. ALTERNATIVELY, IT CAN BE SERVED AS A VEGETABLE ACCOMPANIMENT; IT GOES PARTICULARLY WELL WITH BEEF RENDANG (SEE PAGE 28)

200 g (7 oz) bean sprouts
2 tablespoons groundnut or vegetable oil
1 × 297 g (10.5 oz) packet tofu (bean curd), drained, dried and cut into large dice
1 small onion, chopped finely
3 cloves garlic, chopped finely
2 fresh green chillies, chopped roughly, seeds discarded according to taste
salt
SAUCE:
6 tablespoons water
3 heaped tablespoons crunchy peanut butter
2 tablespoons soy sauce
1-2 tablespoons chilli sauce, according to taste
1 tablespoon black bean sauce
1 tablespoon wine or sherry vinegar
TO GARNISH:
1 tablespoon sesame oil
3 cloves garlic, cut into slivers
matchstick-thin strips of cucumber

Blend the sauce ingredients together in a jug.

Bring a large pan of water to the boil, add the bean sprouts and 1 teaspoon oil and sprinkle over a good pinch of salt. Drain immediately, then return to the pan, cover and keep hot. Heat the wok until hot. Add the remaining oil and heat over a moderate heat until hot. Add the tofu and carefully stir-fry for 1-2 minutes, then lift out with a slotted spoon, drain and keep hot on kitchen paper.

Add the onion, garlic and chillies to the oil in the wok and stir-fry over a gentle heat for 2-3 minutes to blend the flavours without browning the ingredients. Pour in the sauce mixture and bring to the boil over a high heat, stirring constantly until thickened.

Gently toss the bean sprouts and tofu together, then turn into a warmed serving dish and pour over the sauce.

Quickly clean and dry the wok and make the garnish: add the sesame oil, heat over a moderate heat until hot but not smoking, then add the slivers of garlic. Stir-fry for a few seconds until browned. Drizzle the oil and garlic over the peanut sauce and garnish with the cucumber strips. Serve at once.

SERVES 4

Nutritional content per serving: Carbohydrate: 7   Fat: 16   Fibre: 3   Kilocalories: 200

Tahu Goreng; Oriental Vegetable Stir-Fry

ORIENTAL VEGETABLE STIR-FRY

THE COMBINATION OF FRESH VEGETABLES AND TOFU (BEAN CURD) MAKES THIS A NUTRITIOUS VEGETARIAN MAIN COURSE, ESPECIALLY IF SERVED WITH BROWN RICE

2 teaspoons cornflour

8 tablespoons cold vegetable stock or water

3 tablespoons soy sauce

2 star anise

2 tablespoons groundnut or vegetable oil

1 small onion, sliced thinly

125 g (4 oz) green beans, cut into 4 cm (1½ inch) lengths

2 celery sticks, sliced thinly on the diagonal

½ each red, yellow and green peppers, cut into 4 cm (1½ inch) strips

125 g (4 oz) piece mooli, peeled and cut into thin 4 cm (1½ inch) strips

2.5 cm (1 inch) piece fresh root ginger, peeled and crushed

1 clove garlic, crushed

1 × 297 g (10. 5 oz) packet tofu (bean curd), drained, dried and cut into 4 cm (1½ inch) strips

Blend the cornflour in a jug with 2 tablespoons of the stock or water, then add the remaining stock or water, the soy sauce and star anise. Stir well to combine.

Heat the wok until hot. Add half of the oil and heat over a moderate heat until hot. Add the onion and beans and stir-fry for 2 minutes. Add the celery and stir-fry for 2 minutes, then add the peppers and mooli and stir-fry for a further 2 minutes. Remove from the wok and set aside.

Heat the remaining oil in the wok, add the ginger and garlic and stir-fry over a gentle heat for 2-3 minutes to blend the flavours without browning the ingredients. Pour in the cornflour mixture and bring to the boil over a high heat, stirring constantly until thickened and glossy. Discard the star anise. Return the vegetables to the wok, toss over a high heat, then add the tofu and stir-fry for 2-3 minutes until heated through and evenly combined with the vegetables. Serve at once.

SERVES 4

Nutritional content per serving: Carbohydrate: 12   Fat: 11   Fibre: 3   Kilocalories: 180

SZECHUAN AUBERGINE

2 tablespoons groundnut or vegetable oil

I × 375 g (12 oz) aubergine, cut lengthways into 5 mm (¼ inch) thick slices, each slice cut crossways into 5 mm (¼ inch) strips

I cm (½ inch) piece fresh root ginger, peeled and cut into thin slivers

I clove garlic, cut into thin slivers

I green chilli, chopped finely, seeds discarded according to taste

2 spring onions, cut into 5 cm (2 inch) matchsticks

I tablespoon cider vinegar

I teaspoon sesame oil

SAUCE:

2 tablespoons vegetable stock or water

I tablespoon soy sauce

I teaspoon yellow bean sauce

I teaspoon sugar

Blend the sauce ingredients together in a jug.

Heat the wok until hot. Add the groundnut or vegetable oil and heat over a moderate heat until hot. Add the aubergine strips and stir-fry for 30-45 seconds. Remove with a slotted spoon and set aside.

Add the ginger, garlic and chilli, stir-fry for a few seconds to blend the flavours without browning the ingredients, then pour in the sauce ingredients and bring to the boil over a high heat until thickened, stirring constantly.

Return the aubergine strips to the wok and stir-fry for 2 minutes. Add the spring onions and toss to combine. Sprinkle over the vinegar and sesame oil and serve at once.

SERVES 4

Nutritional content per serving: Carbohydrate: 6   Fat: 9   Fibre: 3   Kilocalories: 110

STIR-FRIED SPRING GREENS WITH RAISINS AND PINE KERNELS

THIS DISH CAN EQUALLY WELL BE MADE WITH FRESH SPINACH, IN WHICH CASE THE BLANCHING OF THE LEAVES SHOULD BE OMITTED

350 g (12 oz) spring greens

2 tablespoons walnut or olive oil

I tablespoon butter or margarine

50 g (2 oz) pine kernels

125 g (4 oz) raisins

salt and pepper

Remove the stalks and any tough ribs from the spring greens. Put several leaves one on top of another, roll them up together, tightly, into a cigar shape, then cut crossways into shreds. Repeat with the remaining leaves.

Bring a large saucepan of water to the boil, add salt to taste, then add the shredded spring greens. Bring the water back to the boil and blanch for I minute only, then drain immediately and refresh under cold running water.

Heat the wok until hot. Add the oil and butter or margarine and heat over a moderate heat until foaming. Add the pine kernels and raisins and stir-fry for 2-3 minutes, then add the spring greens and increase the heat to high. Stir-fry for 2-3 minutes until the spring greens are hot, sprinkle with salt and pepper to taste and serve at once.

SERVES 4

Nutritional content per serving: Carbohydrate: 25   Fat: 17   Fibre: 4   Kilocalories: 255

Szechuan Aubergine; Stir-Fried Spring Greens with Raisins and Pine Kernels (bottom); Vegetable Chow Mein

VEGETABLE CHOW MEIN

1 × 250 g (8.82 oz) packet fine egg noodles
2 tablespoons sesame oil
2 carrots, cut into matchsticks
1 green pepper, cored, deseeded and diced
3 celery sticks, sliced thinly on the diagonal
1 × 230 g (8 oz) can water chestnuts, drained and sliced thinly
175 g (6 oz) Chinese leaves, shredded
175 g (6 oz) fresh spinach leaves, shredded
salt and pepper
SAUCE:
2 teaspoons cornflour
4 tablespoons cold vegetable stock or water
2 tablespoons soy sauce
1 tablespoon dry sherry or sherry vinegar

Prepare the sauce: blend the cornflour in a jug with 2 tablespoons of the stock or water, then add the remaining stock or water and the remaining sauce ingredients. Stir well to combine.

Break the noodles up slightly, then cook according to packet instructions. Meanwhile, heat the wok until hot, add the sesame oil and heat over a moderate heat until hot but not smoking.

Add the carrots, green pepper, celery and water chestnuts and stir-fry for 2-3 minutes. Add the Chinese leaves and spinach and stir-fry for 1 minute. Pour in the sauce mixture and bring to the boil over a high heat, stirring constantly until thickened and glossy. Remove from the heat.

Drain the noodles and add to the vegetables. Return the wok to a high heat and toss the ingredients together until evenly combined. Add salt and pepper to taste and serve at once.

SERVES 4

Nutritional content per serving: Carbohydrate: 60 Fat: 13 Fibre: 10 Kilocalories: 390

CRISPY SEAWEED

THIS POPULAR STARTER IN CHINESE RESTAURANTS IS IN FACT USUALLY MADE FROM SPRING GREENS RATHER THAN SEAWEED, AND YOU CAN HARDLY TELL THE DIFFERENCE. IT IS SIMPLICITY ITSELF TO PREPARE AT HOME

375 g (12 oz) spring greens
vegetable oil for deep frying
2 teaspoons caster sugar
1 teaspoon Chinese five-spice powder
¼ teaspoon salt

Remove the stalks and any tough ribs from the spring greens. Put several leaves one on top of another, roll them up together into a cigar shape, then cut crossways into very fine shreds. Repeat with the remaining leaves, then spread the shreds out on a tray to dry.

When ready to cook, pour enough oil into the wok for deep frying and heat to 190°C, 375°F or until a cube of bread browns in 30 seconds. Pick up a good handful of the 'seaweed' shreds and drop them into the hot oil. Deep fry for about 2 minutes or until crisp. Remove with a large slotted spoon and drain on kitchen paper while deep frying the remainder.

When all the shreds are cooked, toss them in a large bowl with the sugar, five-spice powder and salt. Serve warm or cold.

SERVES 4

Nutritional content per serving: Carbohydrate: 5   Fat: 19   Fibre: 2   Kilocalories: 190

THREE-COLOURED PEPPERS

1 tablespoon groundnut or vegetable oil
2 celery sticks, cut into matchsticks
3 small peppers (1 red, 1 green, 1 yellow), cored, deseeded and cut lengthways into matchsticks
2 courgettes, cut into matchsticks
50 g (2 oz) pecan nuts, chopped finely
DRESSING:
2 tablespoons lime juice
1 tablespoon olive oil
1 tablespoon anise-flavoured liqueur
1 clove garlic, crushed
salt and pepper

Combine the dressing ingredients in a large bowl. Heat the wok until hot. Add the oil and heat over a moderate heat until hot. Add the celery and stir-fry for 2 minutes, then add the peppers and stir-fry for 1 minute. Add the courgettes and stir-fry for 2-3 minutes.

Transfer the vegetables to the bowl of dressing and toss well to mix. Cover and chill in the refrigerator for 2 hours. Serve chilled, sprinkled with the chopped pecans.

SERVES 4

Nutritional content per serving: Carbohydrate: 4   Fat: 14   Fibre: 3   Kilocalories: 160

Three-Coloured Peppers; Crispy Seaweed (top); Baby Vegetable Stir-Fry with Orange and Oyster Sauce

BABY VEGETABLE STIR-FRY WITH ORANGE AND OYSTER SAUCE

2 tablespoons olive or walnut oil
175 g (6 oz) baby carrots
175 g (6 oz) whole baby sweetcorn cobs
175 g (6 oz) small button mushrooms
salt and pepper
parsley sprigs to garnish
SAUCE:
2 teaspoons cornflour
4 tablespoons water
finely grated rind and juice of 1 large orange
2 tablespoons oyster sauce
1 tablespoon dry sherry or sherry vinegar

Prepare the sauce: blend the cornflour in a jug with the water, then add the orange rind and juice, oyster sauce and sherry or vinegar. Stir well to combine.

Heat the wok until hot. Add the oil and heat over a moderate heat until hot but not smoking. Add the carrots and sweetcorn and stir-fry for 5 minutes, then add the mushrooms and stir-fry for 3-4 minutes.

Pour in the sauce mixture and bring to the boil over a high heat, stirring constantly until thickened and glossy. Add salt and pepper to taste, garnish with parsley and serve at once.

SERVES 4-6

Nutritional content per serving:　Carbohydrate: 5　Fat: 8　Fibre: 5　Kilocalories: 105

HOT TOSSED GREEN VEGETABLES

375 g (12 oz) broccoli, florets separated,
 stalks sliced thinly on the diagonal
2 tablespoons olive oil
2 medium leeks, white part sliced thinly on
 the diagonal
1 bulb fennel, sliced thinly
2 cloves garlic, cut into thin slivers
2 tablespoons crushed fennel seeds
splash of anise flavoured liqueur
salt and pepper

Blanch the broccoli in boiling salted water for 2 minutes. Drain and rinse under cold running water.

Heat the wok until hot. Add the oil and heat over a moderate heat until hot but not smoking. Add the leeks, fennel and garlic and stir-fry for 2-3 minutes. Add the broccoli, fennel seeds and liqueur. Increase the heat to high and stir-fry for 1 minute or until the broccoli is hot. Add salt and pepper to taste and serve at once.

SERVES 4

Nutritional content per serving: Carbohydrate: 7 Fat: 9 Fibre: 5 Kilocalories: 125

WILTED SPINACH

250 g (8 oz) fresh spinach leaves
1 star anise
2 tablespoons sesame seeds
1 tablespoon sesame oil
2 cloves garlic, crushed
1 teaspoon soy sauce
salt and pepper
parsley sprigs to garnish

Remove the stalks and any tough ribs from the spinach. Put several spinach leaves one on top of another, roll them up together into a cigar shape, then cut crossways into shreds. Repeat with the remaining leaves. Pound the star anise in a pestle and mortar or use the end of a straight wooden rolling pin.

Heat the wok until hot. Add the sesame seeds and dry-fry for 1-2 minutes until golden brown. Transfer to a bowl and set aside.

Heat the oil in the wok over a moderate heat until hot but not smoking. Add the crushed garlic and star anise and stir-fry over gentle heat for 1-2 minutes to flavour the oil. Add the spinach, increase the heat to high and stir-fry for 2 minutes until just wilted. Sprinkle over the soy sauce and sesame seeds, add salt and pepper to taste and mix well. Garnish with parsley sprigs and serve at once.

SERVES 2

Nutritional content per serving: Carbohydrate: 5 Fat: 8 Fibre: 5 Kilocalories: 100

Wilted Spinach; Hot Tossed Green Vegetables (top); Mangetout with Cream and Herbs

MANGETOUT WITH CREAM AND HERBS

2 tablespoons olive oil
2 tablespoons butter or margarine
500 g (1 lb) mangetout
2 cloves garlic, crushed
½ teaspoon granulated sugar
125 ml (4 fl oz) double cream
3 tablespoons chopped fresh herbs
salt and pepper

Heat the wok until hot. Add the oil and butter or margarine and heat over a moderate heat until foaming. Add the mangetout, garlic and sugar and stir-fry for 2-3 minutes. Lift out with a slotted spoon and keep hot in a warmed serving dish.

Add the cream to the wok and bring to the boil, stirring. Boil for a few minutes until thickened, then remove from the heat and stir in the herbs and salt and pepper to taste. Pour over the mangetout and serve at once.

SERVES 4

Nutritional content per serving: Carbohydrate: 5   Fat: 29   Fibre: 5   Kilocalories: 290

CRUNCHY SWEET AND SOUR VEGETABLES

2 tablespoons groundnut or vegetable oil
2 medium carrots, sliced thinly on the
   diagonal
1 head fennel, sliced thinly, reserving leaves
   for garnish
1 red pepper, cored, deseeded and cut into
   1 cm (½ inch) squares
1 green pepper, cored, deseeded and cut into
   1 cm (½ inch) squares
75 g (3 oz) unsalted cashew kernels
½ × 160 g (5 oz) jar sweet and sour sauce
1 × 227 g (8 oz) can pineapple slices in
   natural juice, drained and cut into chunks

Heat the wok until hot. Add the oil and heat over a moderate heat until hot. Add the carrots, fennel, peppers and nuts. Stir-fry for 2 minutes, then add the sweet and sour sauce. Bring to the boil, stirring, then add the pineapple chunks and stir-fry for 2 minutes more, until the pineapple is hot. Serve at once, sprinkled with the reserved fennel leaves.

SERVES 4

Nutritional content per serving: Carbohydrate: 23   Fat: 17   Fibre: 5   Kilocalories: 250

GLAZED CARROTS WITH CORIANDER AND LIME

25 g (1 oz) butter or margarine
1 small onion, chopped finely
1 teaspoon coriander seeds, crushed
500 g (1 lb) carrots, cut into matchsticks
300 ml (½ pint) hot chicken or
   vegetable stock
juice of 1 lime
1 teaspoon soft brown sugar
2 tablespoons finely chopped fresh coriander
salt and pepper

Melt half of the butter or margarine in the wok, add the onion and stir-fry for 2-3 minutes until slightly softened. Add the crushed coriander seeds and the carrots and toss to coat, then add the stock, lime juice, sugar and salt and pepper to taste. Bring to the boil and stir-fry for 5-6 minutes or until the carrots are tender-crisp and the liquid has been absorbed.

Add the remaining butter or margarine, increase the heat to high and stir-fry until the carrots become glazed. Remove from the heat and stir in the fresh coriander. Serve at once.

SERVES 4-6

Nutritional content per serving: Carbohydrate: 9   Fat: 5   Fibre: 4   Kilocalories: 90

Crunchy Sweet and Sour Vegetables; Glazed Carrots with Coriander and Lime (bottom); Mangetout with Ginger and Mint

MANGETOUT WITH GINGER AND MINT

2 tablespoons olive or walnut oil
5 cm (2 inch) piece fresh root ginger, cut into
  matchsticks
500 g (1 lb) mangetout
2 teaspoons lemon juice
2 tablespoons chopped fresh mint
salt and pepper
mint sprigs to garnish

Heat the wok until hot. Add the oil and heat over a moderate heat until hot but not smoking. Add the ginger and stir-fry over gentle heat for 1-2 minutes to flavour the oil.

Add the mangetout and stir-fry for 2 minutes. Remove from the heat and stir in the lemon juice, mint and salt and pepper to taste. Serve at once, garnished with mint sprigs.

SERVES 4-6

Nutritional content per serving: Carbohydrate: 4   Fat: 8   Fibre: 5   Kilocalories: 95

STIR-FRIED SPINACH WITH TOFU

375 g (12 oz) fresh spinach leaves
2 tablespoons groundnut or vegetable oil
½ × 297 g (10.5 oz) packet tofu (bean
  curd), drained, dried and cut into cubes
1 clove garlic, crushed
3-4 spring onions, sliced thinly on the
  diagonal
2.5 cm (1 inch) piece fresh root ginger,
  peeled and chopped finely
2 tablespoons soy sauce
½ teaspoon caster sugar

Remove the stalks and any tough ribs from the spinach. Put several spinach leaves one on top of another, roll them up together, tightly, into a cigar shape, then cut crossways into shreds. Repeat with the remaining leaves.

Heat the wok until hot. Add 1 tablespoon oil and heat over a moderate heat until hot. Add the tofu and garlic and stir-fry for 2 minutes. Lift out with a slotted spoon and drain on kitchen paper.

Wipe the wok clean with kitchen paper. Add the remaining oil and heat until hot, then add the onions and ginger and stir-fry over a gentle heat for a few seconds to flavour the oil.

Add the spinach, soy sauce and sugar and stir-fry for 1-2 minutes or until the spinach just begins to wilt, then return the tofu to the wok and stir-fry for a further 30 seconds to heat through. Serve at once.

SERVES 4

Nutritional content per serving: Carbohydrate: 8   Fat: 10   Fibre: 5   Kilocalories: 135

CAULIFLOWER WITH COCONUT SAUCE

½ × 200 g (7 oz) packet creamed coconut
300 ml (½ pint) boiling water
1 cauliflower, florets separated, stalks sliced
  thinly on the diagonal
1 tablespoon groundnut or vegetable oil
1 onion, chopped finely
2.5 cm (1 inch) piece fresh root ginger, peeled
  and chopped finely
2 cloves garlic, crushed
2 teaspoons ground coriander
¼-½ teaspoon chilli powder, according to
  taste
¼ teaspoon turmeric
salt

Dissolve the creamed coconut in the boiling water to make coconut milk. Parboil the cauliflower florets and stalks in a large saucepan of boiling salted water for 3 minutes. Drain and rinse under cold running water; set aside.

Heat the wok until hot. Add the oil and heat over a moderate heat until hot. Add the onion, ginger and garlic and stir-fry over a gentle heat for 2-3 minutes to blend the flavours without browning the ingredients.

Add the coriander, chilli powder, turmeric, coconut milk and salt to taste. Bring to the boil and simmer gently for 2-3 minutes until the mixture thickens.

Add the cauliflower and simmer for a further 2-3 minutes until tender-crisp. Taste and add more salt if necessary. Serve at once.

SERVES 4

Nutritional content per serving: Carbohydrate: 4   Fat: 13   Fibre: 2   Kilocalories: 135

Stir-Fried Spinach with Tofu; Cauliflower with Coconut Sauce (bottom); Quick Green Bean Sauté

Quick green bean sauté

2 tablespoons unsalted butter
1 tablespoon olive oil
375 g (12 oz) green beans
3 cloves garlic, crushed
3 tablespoons chopped fresh herbs, such as
  parsley, chives, chervil and thyme
salt and pepper
parsley sprigs to garnish

Heat the wok until hot. Add the butter and oil and heat over a moderate heat until foaming.

Add the beans and garlic and sauté gently for 5-6 minutes until the beans are tender-crisp, stirring frequently. Remove from the heat, add the herbs and salt and pepper to taste and stir well to mix. Garnish with parsley and serve at once.

SERVES 4

Nutritional content per serving: Carbohydrate: 4   Fat: 10   Fibre: 3   Kilocalories: 115

Brussels sprouts with water chestnuts

This Chinese-inspired recipe makes a welcome change at Christmastime as an alternative to the more traditional dish of sprouts with ordinary chestnuts

375 g (12 oz) Brussels sprouts, cross cut at
the base
2 tablespoons clear honey
2 tablespoons soy sauce
2 tablespoons dry sherry or sherry vinegar
25 g (1 oz) butter or margarine
½ × 230 g (8 oz) can water chestnuts,
drained and halved
coarse sea salt and pepper
coriander sprigs to garnish

Place the sprouts in a steamer, grind sea salt to taste over them, then cover and steam for 6 minutes, or until tender-crisp.

Meanwhile, put the honey, soy sauce and sherry or vinegar in the wok. Add the butter or margarine and heat gently until melted, stirring constantly. Bring the mixture to the boil, stirring, then simmer until reduced to a glaze.

Add the sprouts and water chestnuts to the glaze and toss to coat. Add salt and pepper to taste, garnish with coriander and serve at once.

SERVES 4

Nutritional content per serving:	Carbohydrate: 14	Fat: 6	Fibre: 7	Kilocalories: 130

Ribbon vegetable stir-fry

Peeling whole vegetables into 'ribbon' shapes is an attractive form of presentation. Any kind of vegetable peeler can be used, but for speed, use a swivel-blade peeler

2 tablespoons olive, walnut or vegetable oil
250 g (8 oz) carrots, peeled into ribbons
250 g (8 oz) courgettes, peeled into ribbons
1 red or yellow pepper, cored, deseeded and
cut into matchsticks
2 cloves garlic, crushed
salt and pepper

Heat the wok until hot. Add the oil and heat over a moderate heat until hot but not smoking. Add the vegetables and garlic and stir-fry for 2 minutes. Add salt to taste and plenty of pepper. Serve at once.

SERVES 4

Nutritional content per serving:	Carbohydrate: 7	Fat: 8	Fibre: 3	Kilocalories: 100

Brussels Sprouts with Water Chestnuts; Ribbon Vegetable Stir-Fry (bottom); Carrots with Orange and Cardamom

CARROTS WITH ORANGE AND CARDAMOM

1 tablespoon cardamom pods

2 tablespoons groundnut or vegetable oil

375 g (12 oz) carrots, sliced thinly on the diagonal

5 cm (2 inch) piece fresh root ginger, peeled and chopped finely

2 teaspoons caster sugar

finely grated rind and juice of 1 large orange

2 teaspoons lemon juice

salt

Remove the seeds from the cardamom pods and crush in a pestle and mortar, or use the end of a straight wooden rolling pin.

Heat the wok until hot. Add the oil and heat over a moderate heat until hot. Add the carrots and ginger and stir-fry for 2-3 minutes, then add the crushed cardamom seeds and stir-fry for a few seconds.

Add the sugar, orange rind and juice, lemon juice and salt to taste. Bring to the boil and stir-fry for 1 minute, or until the liquid is reduced. Serve at once.

SERVES 4

Nutritional content per serving:　Carbohydrate: 12　Fat: 8　Fibre: 4　Kilocalories: 115

Velvet noodles

1 × 50 g (2 oz) drum dried sliced mushrooms
6 tablespoons dried chopped red and green
 peppers
1 × 250 g (8.82 oz) packet medium egg
 noodles
2 tablespoons groundnut or vegetable oil
125 g (4 oz) broccoli, florets separated, stalks
 sliced thinly on the diagonal
125 g (4 oz) carrots, cut into matchsticks
2 cloves garlic, crushed
1 tablespoon sesame oil
SAUCE:
6 tablespoons vegetable stock or water
2 tablespoons soy sauce
1 teaspoon Chinese five-spice powder
½ teaspoon ground ginger

Cook the dried mushrooms in boiling water for 10 minutes, according to the instructions on the drum. Soak the dried peppers for 10 minutes. Cook the noodles according to packet instructions. Blend the sauce ingredients in a jug.

Drain the mushrooms, peppers and noodles. Heat the wok until hot. Add the groundnut or vegetable oil and heat over a moderate heat until hot. Add the broccoli and carrots and stir-fry for 3-4 minutes. Add the garlic, drained mushrooms and peppers, then pour in the sauce mixture and bring to the boil over a high heat, stirring constantly.

Add the drained noodles and toss over a high heat until evenly combined with the vegetables and heated through. Serve at once, sprinkled with the sesame oil.

SERVES 4

Nutritional content per serving: Carbohydrate: 58   Fat: 17   Fibre: 6   Kilocalories: 420

Chilli chips

IF YOU HAVE A MANDOLINE SLICER, USE IT TO GET THESE 'CHIPS' REALLY THIN. ALTERNATIVELY, YOU CAN USE A FOOD PROCESSOR WITH A THIN SLICING DISC ATTACHED

500 g (1 lb) even-sized potatoes, sliced
 very thinly
¼ teaspoon salt
¼ teaspoon chilli powder
vegetable oil for deep frying
3-4 large cloves garlic, halved

Place the potato slices in a bowl, cover with cold water and leave to soak for 30 minutes. Mix together the salt and chilli powder.

Pour enough oil into the wok for deep frying and heat to 190°C, 375°F or until a cube of bread browns in 30 seconds. Drain the potato slices, rinse thoroughly, then dry in a clean tea towel.

When the oil is hot, add the garlic, then about one-quarter of the potato slices. Deep fry for 30 seconds or until the potatoes are crisp and golden, then lift out with a slotted spoon. Drain on kitchen paper and keep hot while deep frying the remainder.

When all the potatoes are deep fried, put them into a bag and sprinkle with the chilli salt. Shake the bag well. Serve at once, as a nibble with drinks or as an accompaniment to an oriental-style meal.

SERVES 4

Nutritional content per serving: Carbohydrate: 26   Fat: 15   Fibre: 2   Kilocalories: 240

Chilli Chips; Velvet Noodles (top); Vegetarian Nutty Rice

VEGETARIAN NUTTY RICE

WITH PROTEIN FROM THE CHEESE AND NUTS, THIS EASY STIR-FRY MAKES A QUICK AND NUTRITIOUS MAIN COURSE. SERVE WITH A TOMATO AND ONION SALAD SPRINKLED WITH A TANGY OIL AND VINEGAR DRESSING

250 g (8 oz) long-grain brown rice
2 tablespoons walnut oil
3 spring onions, chopped finely
I red pepper, cored, deseeded and chopped finely
125 g (4 oz) button mushrooms, trimmed and quartered
I small or ½ large cucumber, cut into I cm (½ inch) dice, seeds discarded
125 g (4 oz) frozen peas or petits pois
100 g (3½ oz) unsalted cashew kernels
2 teaspoons lemon juice
salt and pepper
TO GARNISH:
2 spring onions, chopped finely
125 g (4 oz) vegetarian Cheddar cheese, grated

Cook the rice in boiling salted water according to packet instructions.

Heat the wok until hot. Add the oil and heat over a moderate heat until hot but not smoking. Add the prepared vegetables and the frozen peas and stir-fry for 3-4 minutes. Remove from the heat.

Drain the rice if necessary, then add to the wok with the cashew nuts. Toss over a high heat for about I minute or until all the ingredients are evenly combined, then add the lemon juice and salt and pepper to taste. Serve at once, sprinkled with the chopped spring onions and grated cheese.

SERVES 4

Nutritional content per serving: Carbohydrate: 55   Fat: 20   Fibre: 8   Kilocalories: 445

QUICK AND EASY

HANDY STORE CUPBOARD INGREDIENTS TOSSED QUICKLY IN THE WOK TOGETHER WITH JUST A COUPLE OF FRESH OR FROZEN FOODS WILL MAKE A DELICIOUS YET SUBSTANTIAL MEAL IN A MATTER OF MOMENTS. THIS CHAPTER OFFERS A FEW ORIGINAL TASTY SUGGESTIONS.

SPECIAL FRIED RICE

FROZEN STIR-FRY VEGETABLE MIX COMES IN DIFFERENT FLAVOURS: 'CHINESE STYLE WITH BEAN SPROUTS' GOES WELL IN THIS DISH

1 × 125 g (4.41 oz) packet sweet and sour savoury rice

2 tablespoons groundnut or vegetable oil

1 tablespoon butter or margarine

1 clove garlic, crushed

1 × 340 g (12 oz) packet frozen stir-fry vegetable mix

1 × 113 g (4 oz) packet cooked ham slices, shredded

1 tablespoon soy sauce

dash of Tabasco sauce, or to taste

2 hard-boiled eggs, cut into wedges

Cook the savoury rice according to packet instructions.

Meanwhile, heat the wok until hot. Add the oil and butter or margarine and heat over a moderate heat until foaming. Add the garlic and vegetable mix and stir-fry according to packet instructions.

Drain the rice and add to the vegetables with the ham, soy sauce and Tabasco sauce. Increase the heat to high and toss the ingredients together until evenly mixed. Serve at once, topped with the wedges of hard-boiled egg.

SERVES 3-4

Nutritional content per serving: Carbohydrate: 36 Fat: 16 Fibre: 4 Kilocalories: 325

CHINESE CHICKEN

1 tablespoon groundnut or vegetable oil

4 cooked chicken portions, skinned, boned and diced

1 × 198 g (7 oz) can whole kernel sweetcorn, drained

½ teaspoon Chinese five-spice powder

4 tablespoons sweet and sour sauce

1 × 227 g (8 oz) can pineapple slices in natural juice, drained and chopped

Heat the wok until hot. Add the oil and heat over a moderate heat until hot. Increase the heat to high, add the chicken meat, sweetcorn and five-spice powder and toss to combine, then stir in the sweet and sour sauce. Stir-fry until the chicken and sweetcorn are piping hot and evenly mixed, then fold in the pieces of pineapple and heat through. Serve at once.

SERVES 4

Nutritional content per serving: Carbohydrate: 17 Fat: 8 Fibre: 3 Kilocalories: 230

Chinese Chicken (bottom); Special Fried Rice

THREE-BEAN STIR-FRY

THIS IS THE PERFECT STIR-FRY FOR VEGETARIANS. SERVED WITH NUTTY BROWN RICE, THE BEANS AND THE RICE COMBINE TOGETHER TO MAKE A PROTEIN PACKED MEAL

2 tablespoons groundnut or vegetable oil
1 onion, chopped finely
2 garlic cloves, crushed
1 × 432 g (15.2 oz) can borlotti beans, drained and rinsed
1 × 432 g (15.2 oz) can red kidney beans, drained and rinsed
1 × 432 g (15.2 oz) can cannellini beans, drained and rinsed
1 × 397 g (14 oz) can passatta or creamed tomatoes (sieved Italian tomatoes)
2 tablespoons tomato purée
2 teaspoons Worcestershire sauce
1 teaspoon granulated sugar
4 tablespoons chopped fresh parsley
salt and pepper
parsley sprigs to garnish

Heat the wok until hot. Add the oil and heat over a moderate heat until hot. Add the onion and garlic and stir-fry over a gentle heat until the onion has softened slightly.

Add the 3 kinds of beans and increase the heat to high. Toss well to mix then add the passatta or creamed tomatoes a little at a time and stir-fry after each addition until evenly combined with the beans. Add the tomato purée, Worcestershire sauce and sugar, then boil until reduced, stirring constantly. Remove from the heat, stir in the parsley and salt and pepper to taste, garnish with parsley and serve at once.

SERVES 4

Nutritional content per serving: Carbohydrate: 39   Fat: 9   Fibre: 16   Kilocalories: 285

SEAFOOD STIR-FRY

CRAB STICKS ARE INEXPENSIVE AND PERFECTLY SUITED TO STIR-FRIES. THEY RETAIN THEIR SHAPE REALLY WELL AND ARE FULL OF FLAVOUR

2 tablespoons groundnut or vegetable oil
½ onion, chopped finely
1 clove garlic, crushed
1 × 200 g (12 stick) packet frozen crab sticks, sliced on the diagonal
125 g (4 oz) frozen cooked peeled prawns
1 × 350 g (12 oz) packet fresh stir-fry vegetables
1 tablespoon cornflour blended in 2 tablespoons water
2 tablespoons soy sauce
2 tablespoons dry sherry or sherry vinegar
1 tablespoon soft light or dark brown sugar
1 tablespoon chilli sauce (optional)
salt and pepper
parsley sprigs to garnish

Heat the wok until hot. Add the oil and heat over a moderate heat until hot. Add the onion and garlic and stir-fry over a gentle heat to flavour the oil, then add the crab sticks, prawns, stir-fry vegetables and salt and pepper to taste. Increase the heat to high and stir-fry for 3-4 minutes until the shellfish have defrosted.

Mix together the remaining ingredients, add to the wok and bring to the boil over a high heat, stirring constantly until thickened and glossy. Garnish with parsley and serve at once.

SERVES 4

Nutritional content per serving: Carbohydrate: 19   Fat: 9   Fibre: 4   Kilocalories: 225

Seafood Stir-Fry (bottom); Three-Bean Stir-Fry

BUDDHA'S POT

FOR THIS RECIPE, YOU CAN USE STIR-FRY VEGETABLE MIX WITH TROPICAL FRUITS AND ALMONDS. IT'S A QUICK AND EASY WAY TO ADD INTEREST AND EXTRA FLAVOUR TO SIMPLE YET NUTRITIOUS INGREDIENTS LIKE TOFU (BEAN CURD) AND CHINESE LEAVES

2 tablespoons groundnut or vegetable oil
1 × 297 g (10.5 oz) packet tofu (bean
　curd), drained, dried and cut into cubes
1 tablespoon butter or margarine
1 × 340 g (12 oz) packet frozen stir-fry
　vegetable mix of your choice
250 g (8 oz) Chinese leaves, shredded
2 tablespoons soy sauce
2 teaspoons lemon juice
salt and pepper
basil sprigs to garnish

Heat the wok until hot. Add the oil and heat over a moderate heat until hot. Add the tofu cubes and stir-fry for 2-3 minutes until lightly coloured on all sides. Remove with a slotted spoon. Drain and keep warm on kitchen paper.

　　Add the butter or margarine to the oil in the wok and heat until foaming. Add the frozen vegetable mix and cook according to packet instructions, then add the Chinese leaves, soy sauce, lemon juice and salt and pepper to taste. Increase the heat to high and stir-fry for 2-3 minutes until all the ingredients are hot and evenly combined. Add the tofu, fold in gently and serve at once garnished with basil.

SERVES 4

Nutritional content per serving:　Carbohydrate: 13　Fat: 14　Fibre: 4　Kilocalories: 215

THAI-FRIED NOODLES WITH PRAWNS

THIS IS A VERSION OF A TASTY SNACK ENJOYED BY THAI CHILDREN WHEN THEY RETURN HOME FROM SCHOOL. IT CAN BE MADE WITH ANY LEFTOVER MEAT, BACON OR HAM INSTEAD OF THE PRAWNS USED HERE

1 × 250 g (8.82 oz) packet Italian egg
　vermicelli
2 tablespoons groundnut or vegetable oil
125 g (4 oz) radishes, thinly sliced
4 tablespoons lemon juice
1 tablespoon caster sugar
2 teaspoons anchovy extract
¼-½ teaspoon chilli powder, according to
　taste
125-175 g (4-6 oz) peeled cooked prawns,
　drained and thoroughly dried if frozen
dill sprigs to garnish

Cook the vermicelli according to packet instructions.

　　Meanwhile, heat the wok until hot. Add the oil and heat over a moderate heat until hot. Add the radishes, increase the heat to high and stir-fry for 30 seconds. Add the lemon juice, sugar, anchovy extract and chilli powder. Stir-fry for 1-2 minutes until all of the ingredients are evenly combined, then add the prawns and stir-fry for 30 seconds or until heated through.

　　Drain the vermicelli and add to the prawn mixture. Toss the ingredients over a high heat until evenly mixed. Garnish with dill sprigs and serve at once.

SERVES 3-4

Nutritional content per serving:　Carbohydrate: 25　Fat: 7　Fibre: 2　Kilocalories: 180

Thai-Fried Noodles with Prawns (bottom); Buddha's Pot

SCRAMBLED EGG AND HAM BREAKFAST

1 tablespoon butter or margarine
250 g (8 oz) button mushrooms, thinly sliced
250 g (8 oz) tomatoes, roughly chopped
2 tablespoons groundnut or vegetable oil
1 bunch spring onions, shredded
5 eggs, beaten with salt and pepper
1 × 113 g (4 oz) packet cooked ham slices,
    cut into strips
salt and pepper

Heat the wok until hot. Add the butter or margarine and heat over a moderate heat until foaming. Add the mushrooms and stir-fry until the juices run, then add the tomatoes, increase the heat to high and stir-fry for 2-3 minutes. Add salt and pepper to taste. Turn into a warmed serving dish and keep hot.

Add the oil to the wok and heat over a moderate heat until hot. Add half of the spring onions and stir-fry for 1-2 minutes. Pour in the seasoned eggs and stir-fry for 2-3 minutes until softly scrambled. Fold in the strips of ham and heat through. Spoon over the mushroom mixture, garnish with the remaining spring onions and serve at once.

SERVES 4

Nutritional content per serving: Carbohydrate: 2   Fat: 19   Fibre: 3   Kilocalories: 240

HOT-TOSSED NOODLES WITH SPICY MEAT SAUCE

THIS IS AN ORIENTAL VERSION OF SPAGHETTI BOLOGNESE, AND VERY TASTY IT IS TOO!

2 tablespoons groundnut or vegetable oil
1 small onion, chopped finely
500 g (1 lb) minced beef
150 ml (¼ pint) beef stock
2 tablespoons soy sauce
2 tablespoons tomato purée
1 tablespoon sherry vinegar or wine vinegar
½ teaspoon chilli powder, or to taste
½ teaspoon sugar
¼ teaspoon garlic salt
1 × 250 g (8.82 oz) packet medium egg
    noodles
marjoram sprigs to garnish

Heat the wok until hot. Add the oil and heat over a moderate heat until hot. Add the onion and stir-fry over a gentle heat for 2-3 minutes until softened. Add the meat, increase the heat to high and stir-fry for 5 minutes until it loses its pink colour.

Add all of the remaining ingredients except the noodles and bring to the boil, stirring. Lower the heat, cover the wok with a lid and simmer for 10-15 minutes until thickened, stirring frequently.

Meanwhile, cook the noodles according to packet instructions. Drain, then turn into a warmed large bowl.

Add the meat sauce to the noodles and toss quickly to mix. Garnish with marjoram sprigs and serve at once.

SERVES 4

Nutritional content per serving: Carbohydrate: 49   Fat: 33   Fibre: 4   Kilocalories: 620

Scrambled Egg and Ham Breakfast (top); Hot-Tossed Noodles with Spicy Meat Sauce (left); Mandarin Chicken (bottom; see recipe overleaf); Rapid-Fried Mussels with Sweetcorn and Peppers (right; see recipe overleaf)

Rapid-fried mussels with sweetcorn and peppers

1 tablespoon ground or vegetable oil

1 tablespoon butter or margarine

1 × 454 g (1 lb) packet frozen sweetcorn and peppers mix

2 cloves garlic, crushed

1 × 250 g (8 oz) can mussels in brine, drained and rinsed

2 teaspoons cornflour blended with 2 tablespoons water

2 tablespoons soy sauce

2 teaspoons lemon juice

2 tablespoons chopped fresh parsley

salt and pepper

Heat the wok until hot. Add the oil and butter or margarine and heat over a moderate heat until foaming. Add the frozen vegetables and garlic, increase the heat to high and stir-fry for 5-6 minutes.

Add the mussels, cornflour paste, soy sauce, lemon juice and salt and pepper to taste. Bring to the boil over a high heat, stirring constantly until thickened and glossy. Stir in the parsley and serve at once.

SERVES 2

Nutritional content per serving: Carbohydrate: 23   Fat: 9   Fibre: 7   Kilocalories: 230

Mandarin chicken

2 tablespoons groundnut or vegetable oil

3-4 spring onions, roughly chopped

5 cm (2 inch) piece fresh root ginger, peeled and finely chopped

1 clove garlic, crushed

375 g (12 oz) skinned and boned cooked chicken

1 × 298 g (10½ oz) can mandarin oranges in natural juice, drained, with 3 tablespoons juice reserved

salt and pepper

SAUCE:

2 teaspoons cornflour blended with 2 tablespoons cold water

2 tablespoons white wine vinegar

2 tablespoons soy sauce

1 teaspoon soft dark brown sugar

First prepare the sauce: blend all the ingredients in a jug with the reserved 3 tablespoons mandarin juice. Heat the wok until hot. Add the oil and heat over a moderate heat until hot. Add the spring onions, ginger and garlic and stir-fry over a gentle heat to flavour the oil without browning the ingredients. Add the chicken, increase the heat to high and stir-fry for 1-2 minutes until hot.

Pour in the sauce mixture and bring to the boil over a high heat, stirring constantly until thickened and glossy. Add the mandarin segments, stir-fry for 1 minute or until heated through, taking care not to break the segments, then add salt and pepper to taste. Serve at once.

SERVES 2-3

Nutritional content per serving: Carbohydrate: 16   Fat: 11   Fibre: 1   Kilocalories: 250

INDEX

ACKNOWLEDGEMENTS

Series Editor: **Nicola Hill**
Art Editor: **Lee Griffiths**
Designer: **Janet James**
Production Controller: **Alyssum Ross**
Photographer: **James Murphy**
Home Economist: **Allyson Birch**
Stylist: **Marian Price**
Jacket Photographer: **Vernon Morgan**